P·A·P·E·R O·N·L·Y

THE PAPERED PARLOUR

PROJECTS, TEXT AND STYLING BY CLAIRE HEAFFORD
PHOTOGRAPHY BY LOUISE HALL

PAVILION

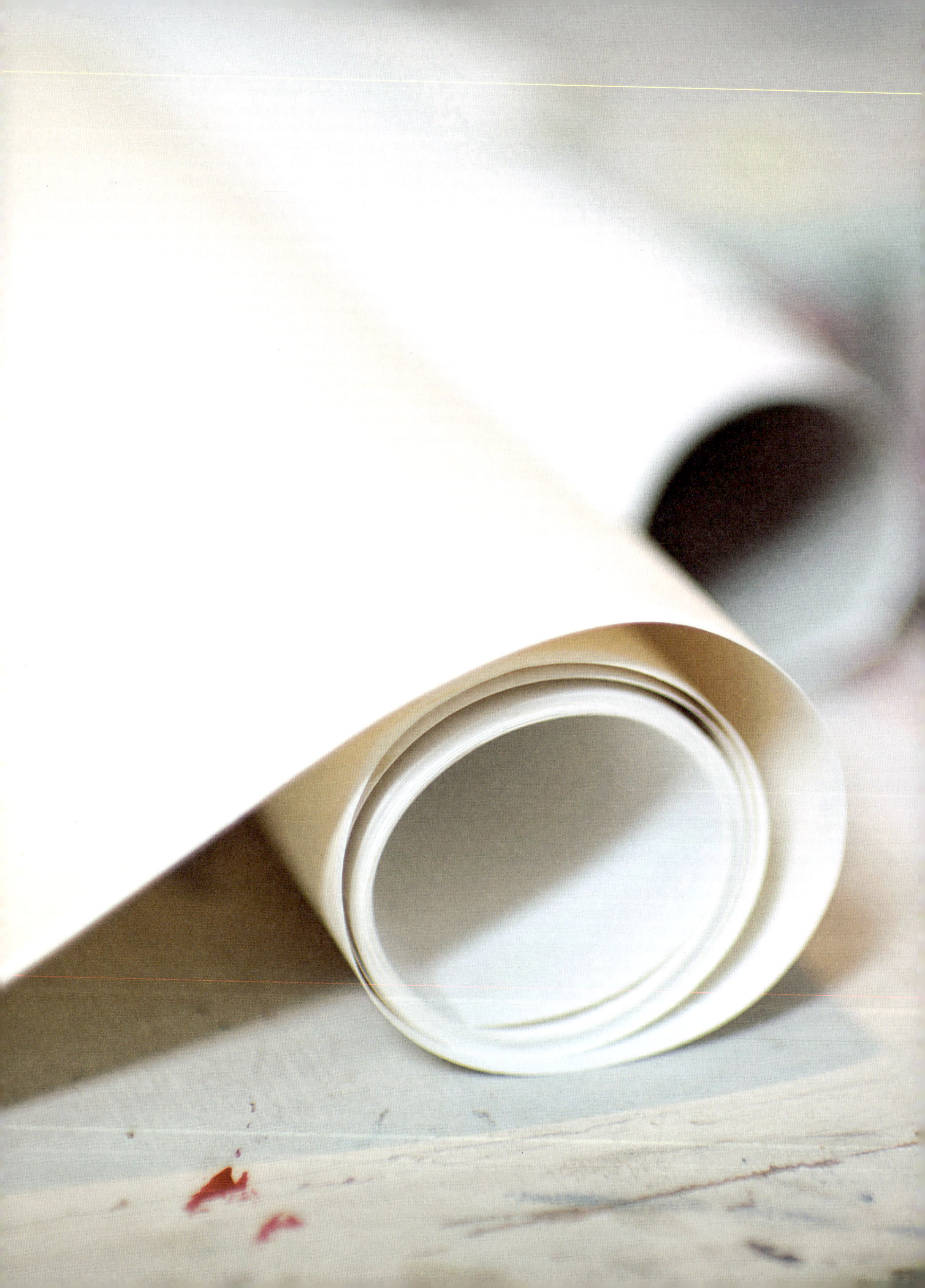

× FOR ARTISTS, WRITERS, DESIGNERS AND MAKERS, THE JOURNEY OF CREATIVITY ALWAYS BEGINS WITH A BLANK SHEET OF PAPER.

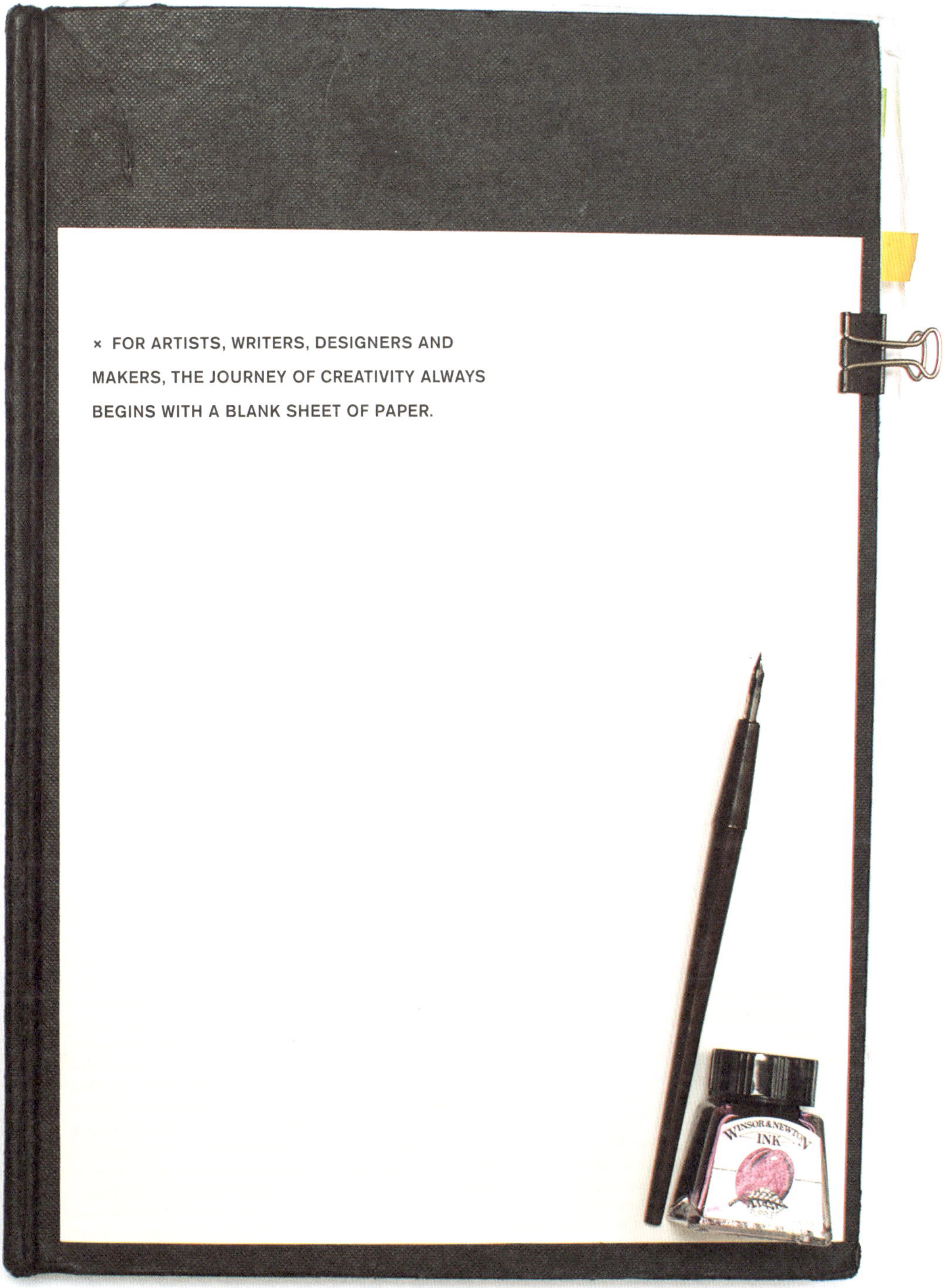

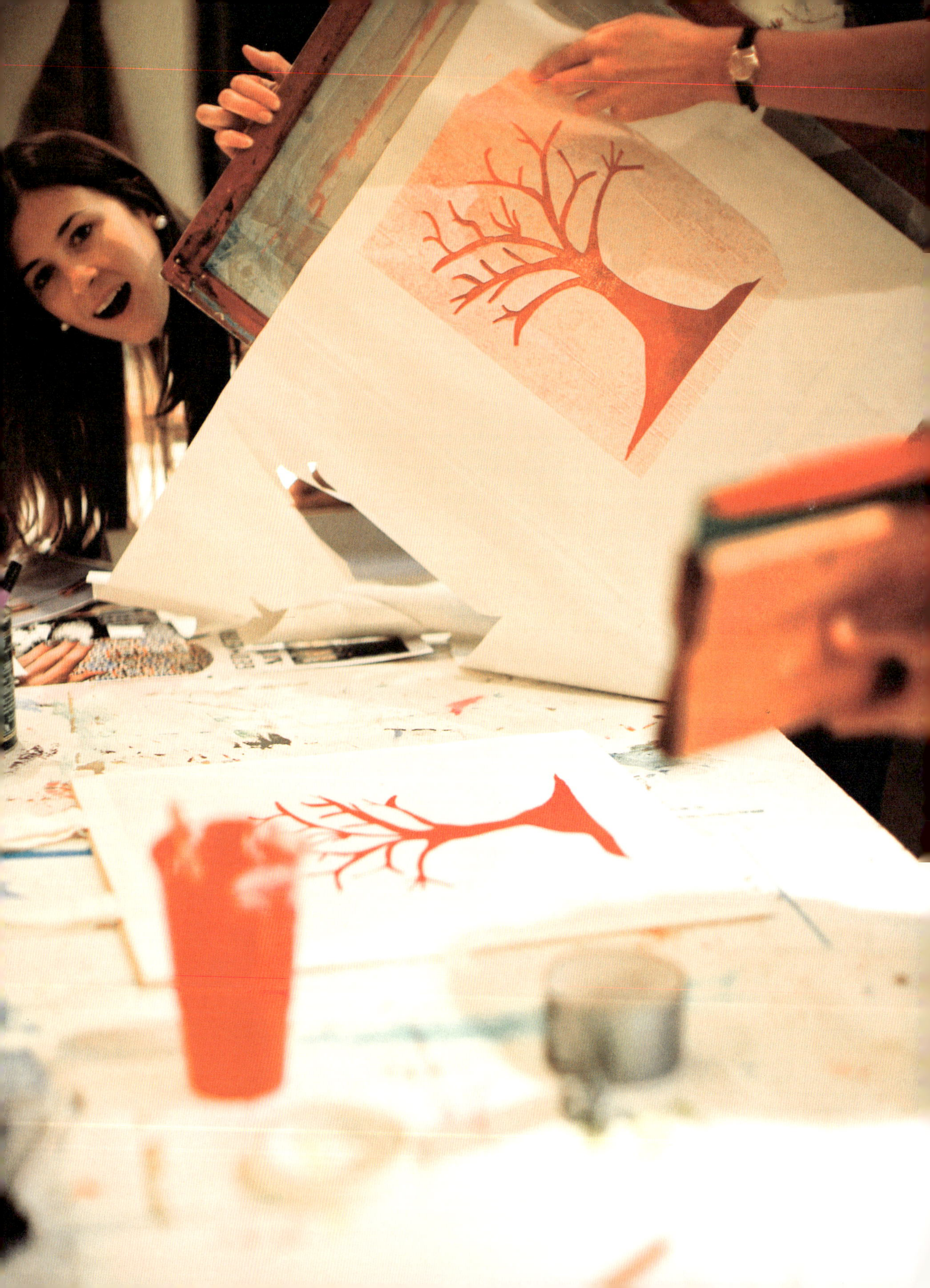

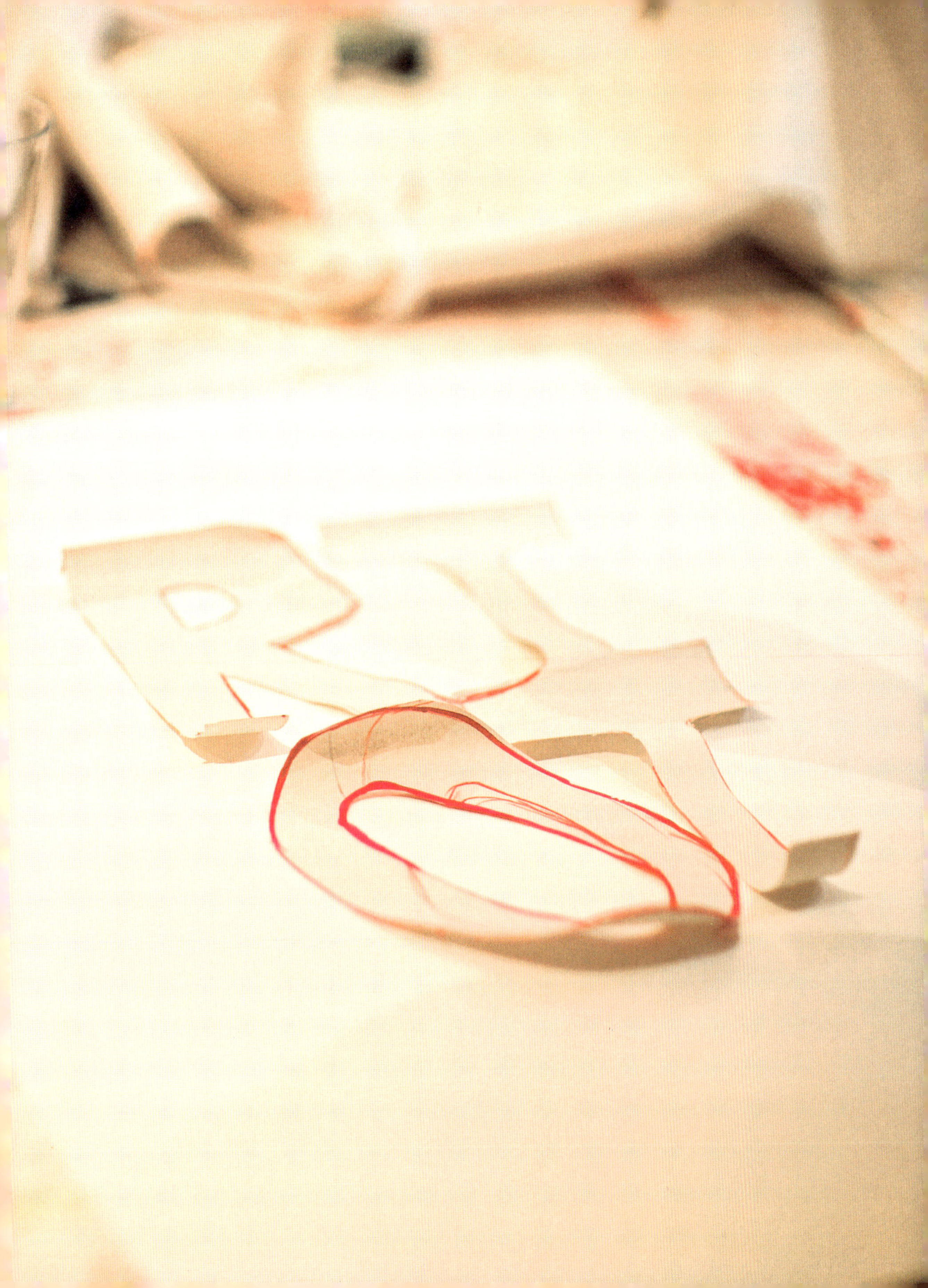

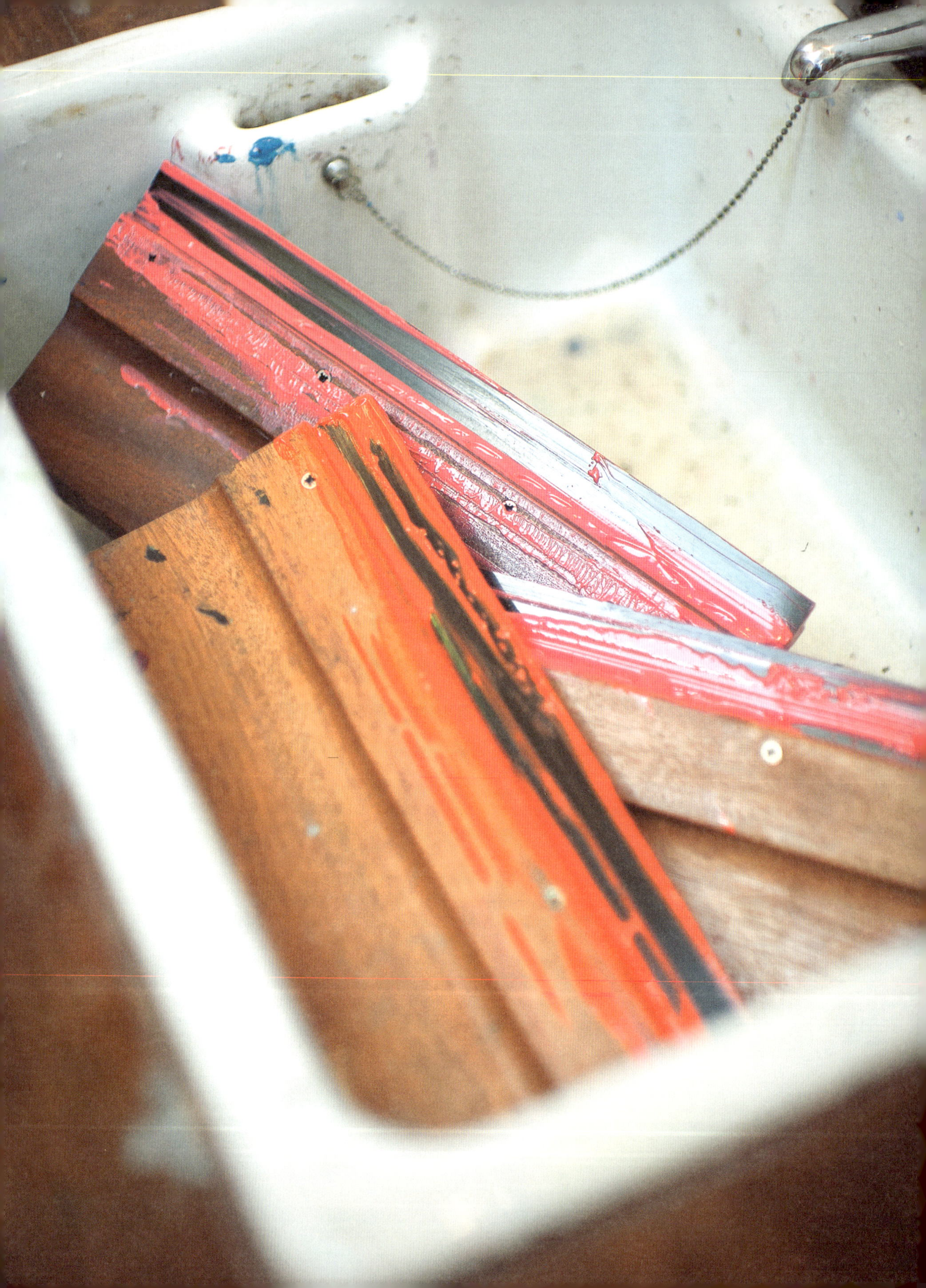

CONTENTS

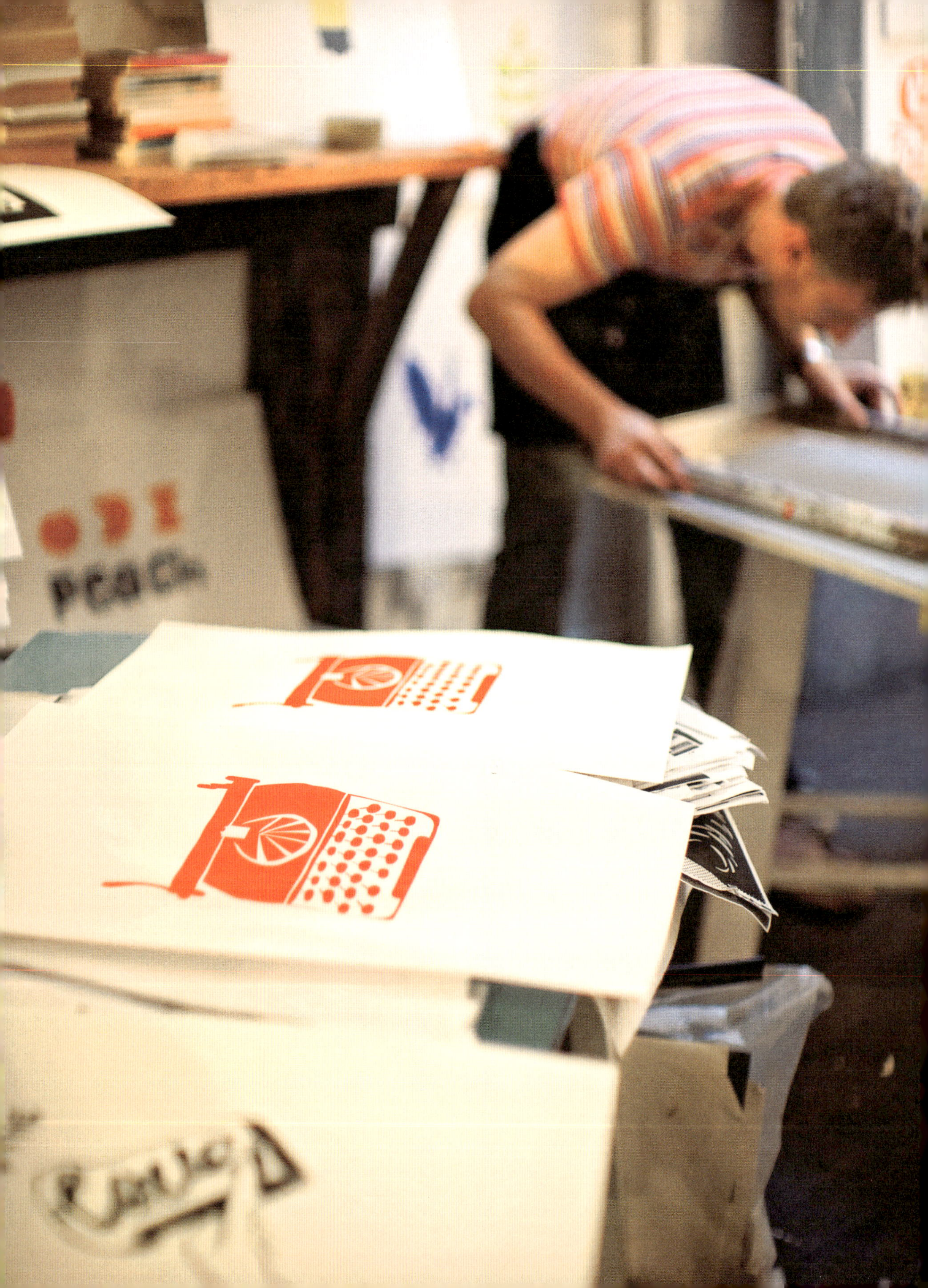

INTRODUCTION

× THIS BOOK IS FOR PEOPLE WHO LOVE TO MAKE: IT CONTAINS 20 PROJECTS YOU CAN MAKE FROM PAPER. BUT *PAPER ONLY* IS NOT JUST A CRAFT BOOK – IT IS A BOOK ABOUT CREATIVITY. SO GET READY TO PUSH PAPER TO ITS LIMITS AND SEE WHERE YOUR CREATIVE JOURNEY TAKES YOU.

Reconnect with the simple joy of paper, paint and glue and join us on an artistic adventure as we cut, fold and stick our way through the fundamentals of art and design. Taking a messy and carefree approach to creativity, you'll be encouraged to scatter your sketchbooks with insights and inspiration, test ideas and take artistic risks. And there's no need to worry – because with paper, if you make a mistake, you can just screw it up and start again.

Offering 20 ways to set your creativity alight, each project includes ideas to help activate your imagination. Some projects are simple exercises to get you started, others ask for a little more time and concentration in exchange for greater creative rewards. In order to help you know where to start, we've come up with three different difficulty ratings:

- Piece of Cake: for easy projects.
- Put Your Thinking Cap On: for projects of medium difficulty.
- Hard Nut to Crack: for trickier projects.

If you're new to making, we suggest you build your confidence slowly by starting with the easier projects. If you've got previous making experience, start where you like – just be sure to read the Parlour Ground Rules (see page 13) before you begin.

By the time you reach the final pages of this book, you'll be armed with the skills and encouragement you need to take making into your own hands. So get ready to follow the paper trail and let your artistic adventure begin.

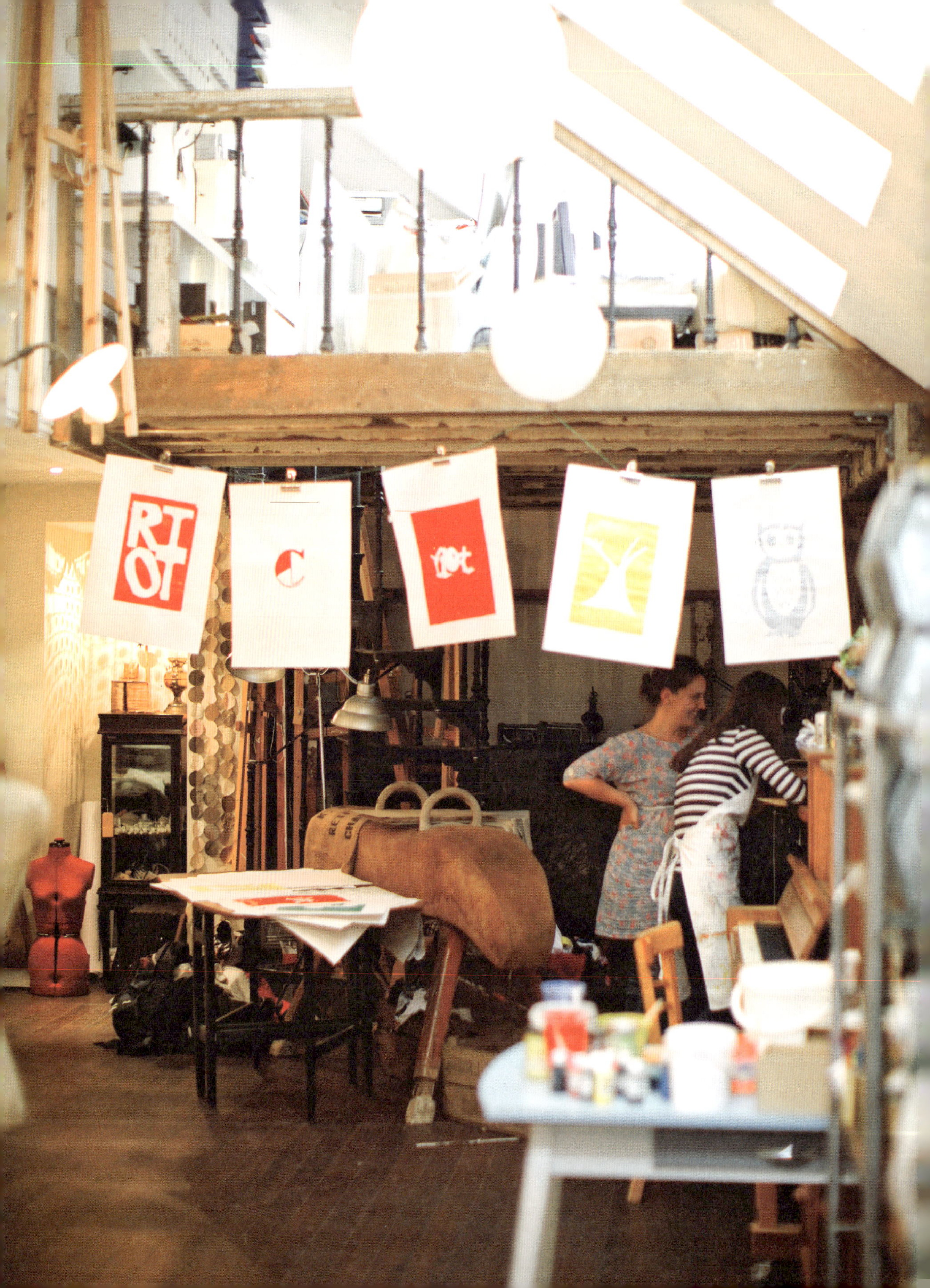

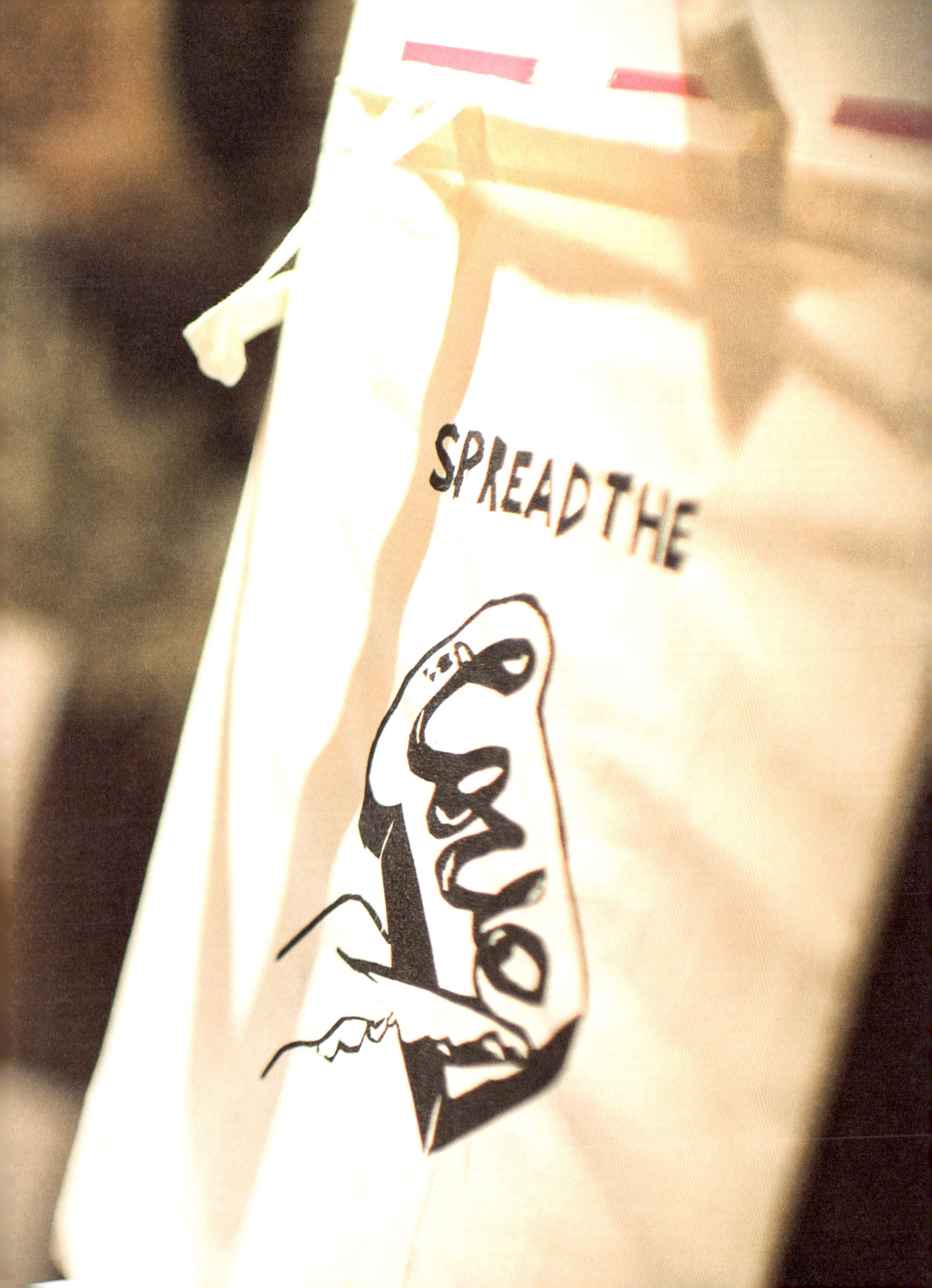
SPREAD THE

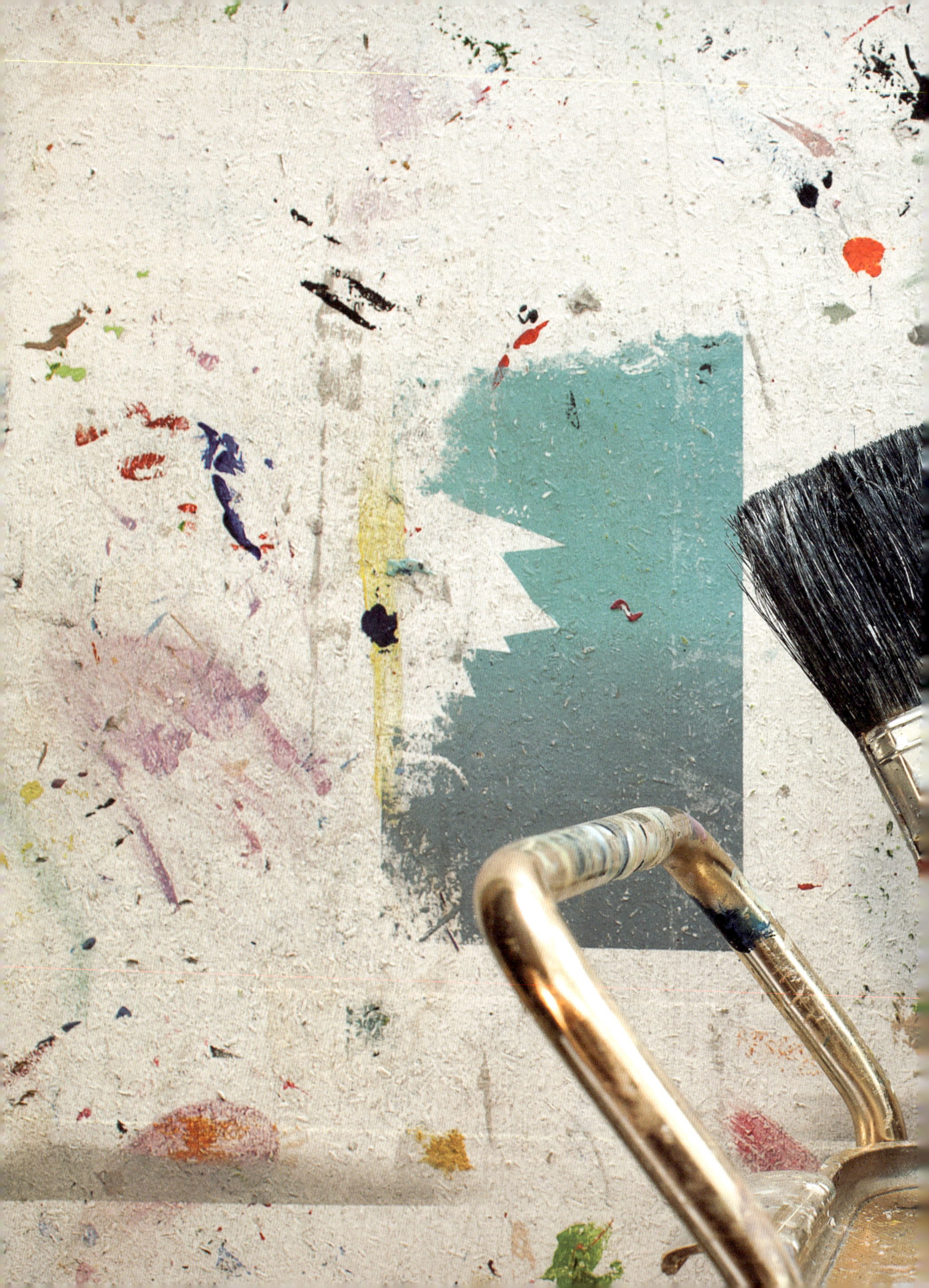

PARLOUR GROUND RULES

1. START RIGHT NOW – START ANYWHERE YOU LIKE, JUST AS LONG AS YOU BEGIN
2. DON'T SPEND MONEY ON EXPENSIVE MATERIALS – USE WHAT YOU HAVE TO HAND
3. EXPERIMENT
4. BE CURIOUS AND PLAYFUL
5. PRACTICE MAKES PERFECT
6. CREATIVITY IS MESSY, THERE'S NO POINT PRETENDING OTHERWISE
7. MISTAKES – HAPPY ACCIDENTS – ARE THE SOURCE OF ALL INNOVATION
8. IF YOU DON'T LIKE WHAT YOU'VE MADE, JUST SCREW IT UP AND START OVER

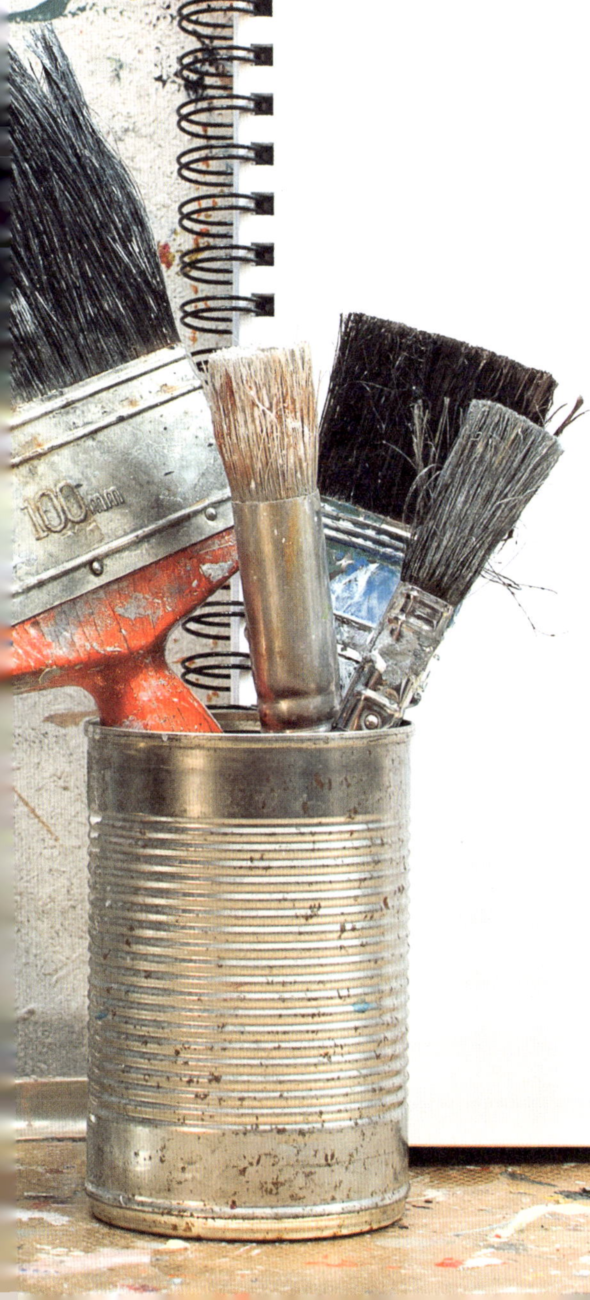

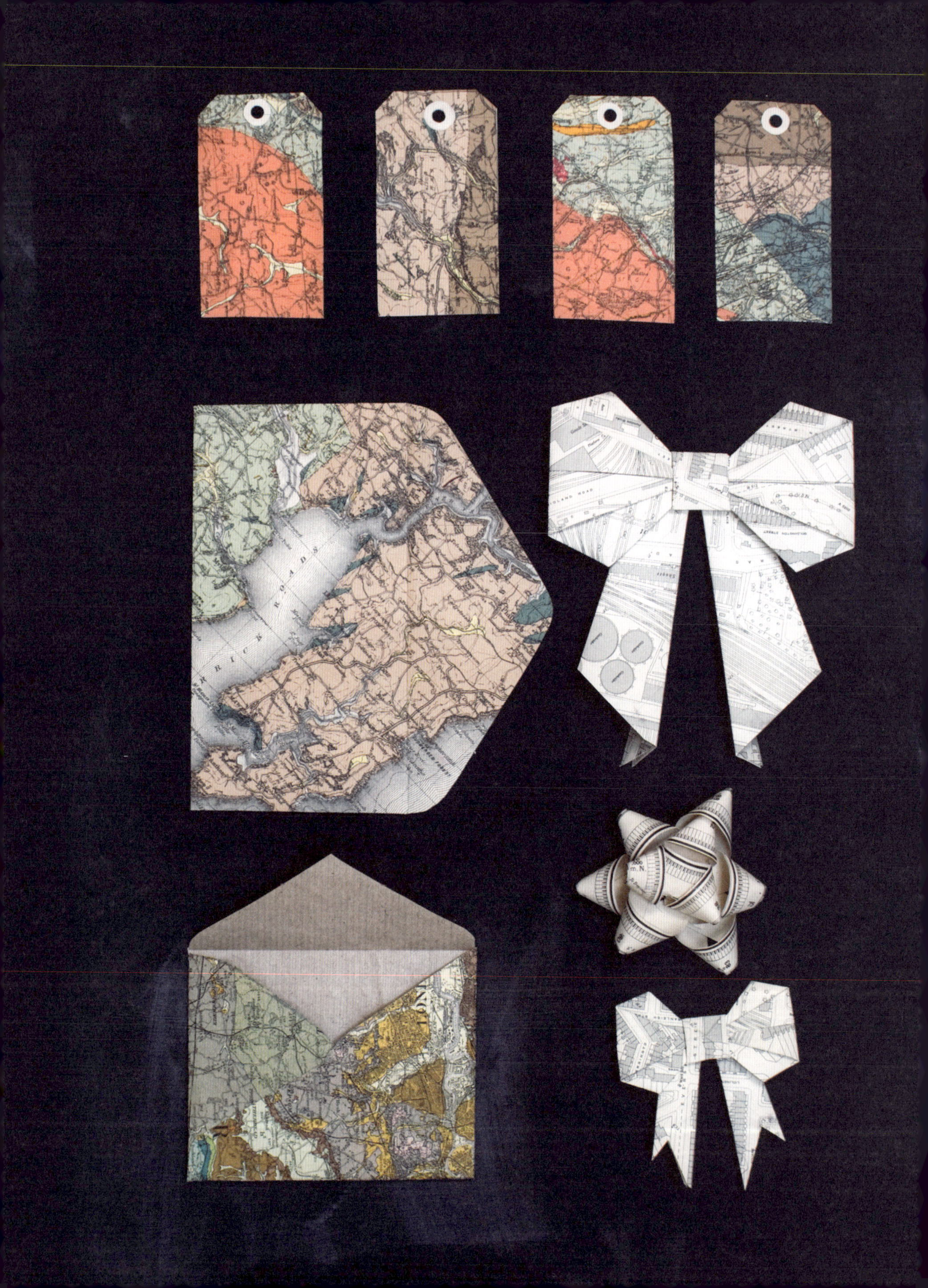

BITS YOU'LL NEED

× **YOU DON'T NEED A DESIGN DEGREE TO GET SOMETHING FROM THIS BOOK – JUST A TINY SPARK OF IMAGINATION AND A FEW BITS OF BASIC KIT WILL DO.**

BASIC TOOLS

× Scissors
× Ruler
× Pencil
× Baker's twine or string
× Hole punch
× Glue gun and glue sticks
× PVA glue
× Dylon dye
× Basic selection of acrylic paints
× Rubber gloves
× Plastic apron
× Paintbrushes
× Washi tape
× Sponge

PRINTING TOOLS

× Printing roller
× Plastic pots
× Plastic tray
× Leftover emulsion paint and tester pots
× Screen-printing medium
× Silkscreen
× Squeegee
× Brown tape
× Polystyrene sheets

SUGGESTED MATERIALS

× Tissue paper
× Old book pages
× Tracing paper
× Newsprint
× Photocopy paper
× Maps
× Sheet music
× Old envelopes
× Brown paper
× Lining paper
× Paper bags
× Cartridge paper
× Postcards
× Watercolour paper
× Cardboard

20 WAYS TO KICK-START YOUR CREATIVITY

1

W·A·R·M U·P

× AS A RAW MATERIAL, PAPER IS VALUED FOR ITS LIGHTNESS, FLEXIBILITY AND VERSATILITY. IT CAN BE TWISTED, TORN, CUT AND CURLED INTO VIRTUALLY ANY SHAPE. ITS SURFACE ABSORBS PAINT AND INK, MAKING IT THE PERFECT MEDIUM FOR WRITING, DRAWING AND PRINTING. IT IS CHEAP, SMOOTH AND OPAQUE — IDEAL FOR USE IN LIGHTING AND INTERIOR DECORATION. DESPITE ITS DIVERSE RANGE OF PROPERTIES, MOST OF US ONLY EVER USE PAPER FOR ORDINARY THINGS — SO TAKE A LITTLE TIME TO GET TO KNOW EXACTLY WHAT PAPER CAN DO AND FIND OUT WHAT IT TAKES TO TURN THE ORDINARY INTO THE EXTRAORDINARY.

Take a sheet of A4 (letter) paper and begin exploring its properties by playing around with the sheet to see what you can do with it. Work your way through the list of words on the right, experimenting and testing the different processes until you have a good idea of where the paper's limits lie. There is no need to try and make a finished product; the aim of the exercise is just to play around until you find a way of working with paper that opens your eyes to its endless possibilities. It may take five minutes or five years – it's up to you.

- × Fold
- × Scrunch
- × Loop
- × Bend
- × Roll
- × Curl
- × Weave
- × Thread
- × Cut
- × Stick
- × Rip
- × Tear
- × Print
- × Draw
- × Write
- × Paint
- × Colour

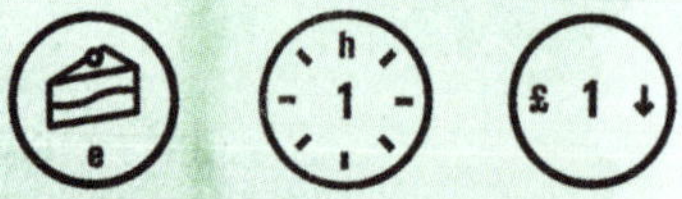

WHAT YOU NEED

- × A few sheets of paper

Cut, fold and stick your way through the fundamentals of art and design

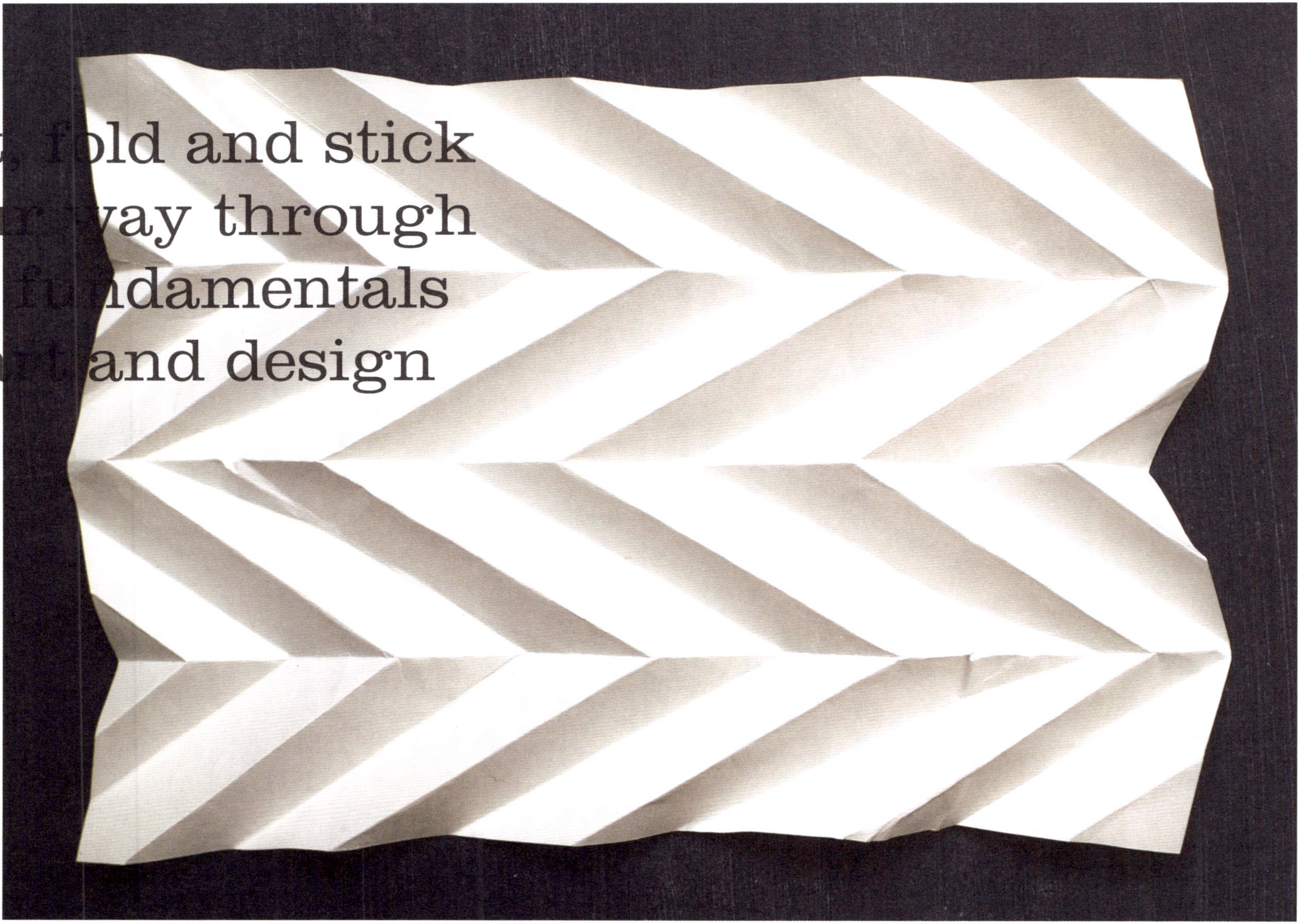

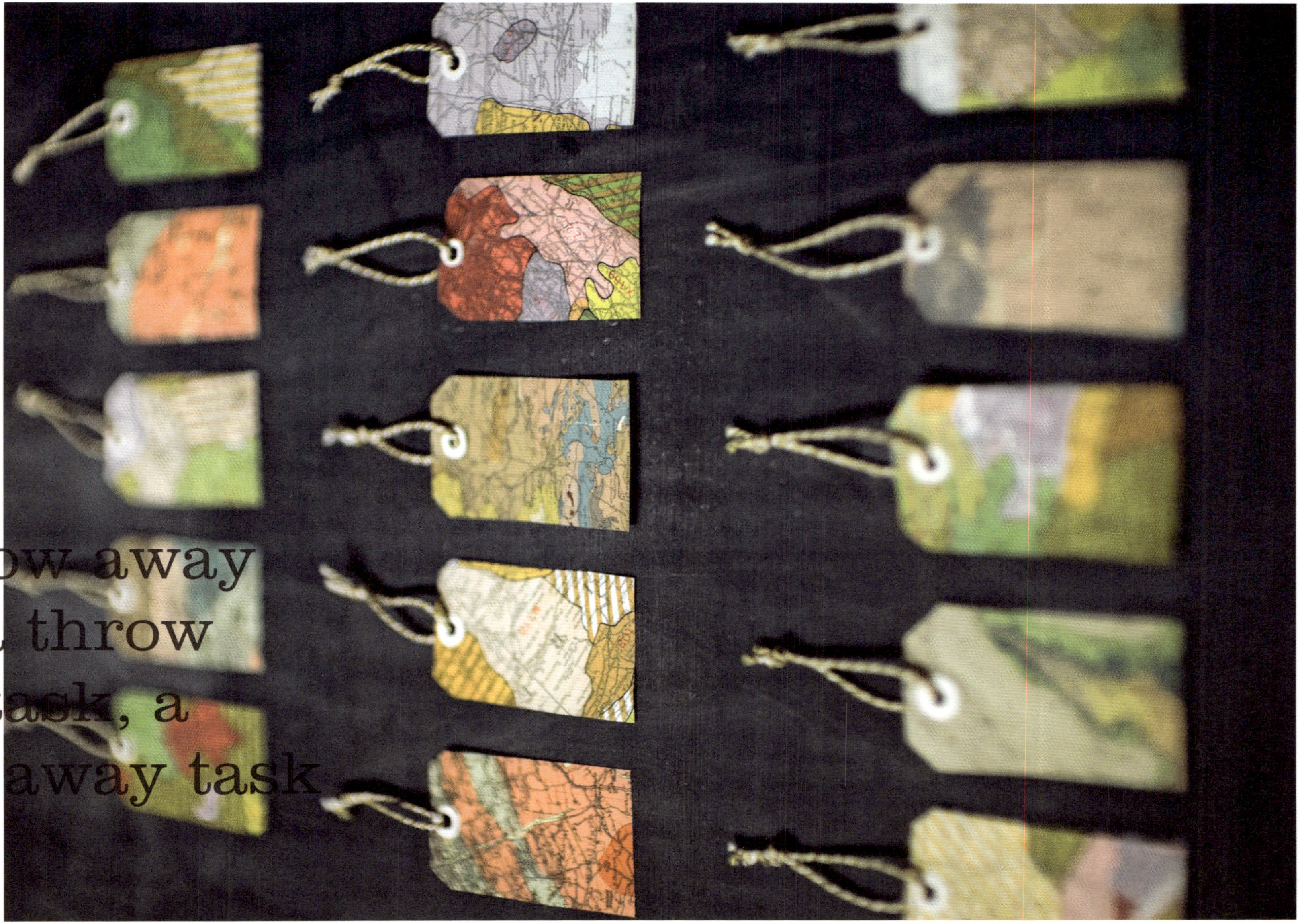

throw away
k, a throw
ay task, a
ow away task

2

G·I·F·T T·A·G·S

× **EVERYONE LOVES THE THRILL OF RECEIVING A GORGEOUS GIFT, SO ADD A DELIGHTFUL DETAIL TO YOUR ELEGANT OFFERINGS – WITH A HANDMADE GIFT TAG.**

WHAT YOU NEED

- × An old map or any other type of paper that will look beautiful as an envelope (sheet music, book pages)
- × Pencil
- × Ruler
- × Hole punch
- × Scissors
- × PVA glue or a glue stick
- × Baker's twine or string

1. Cut out a small rectangle measuring 6 x 10cm ($2\frac{3}{8}$ x 4in) from one corner of the map.

2. Use the hole punch to make a hole at one end of the rectangle. If you don't manage to get the hole in the centre of the tag first time, just trim off the excess from the larger side to make it even again. Then take a bit off the bottom to keep the shape in proportion.

3. Cut the corners closest to the hole off the rectangle. Make sure the angle you cut at is 45 degrees.

4. Take a plain piece of the map and punch another hole, then cut a circle approximately 5mm ($\frac{3}{16}$in) wide around the outside of the hole.

5. Stick the ring of plainer paper over the hole in the tag and secure it with a tiny dab of glue.

6. Thread a 12cm ($4\frac{3}{4}$in) length of baker's twine or string through the holes of the tags and tie knots at the ends.

7. Write a message on a tag and attach it to a gift. Alternatively, hang the tags around the house as decorative details.

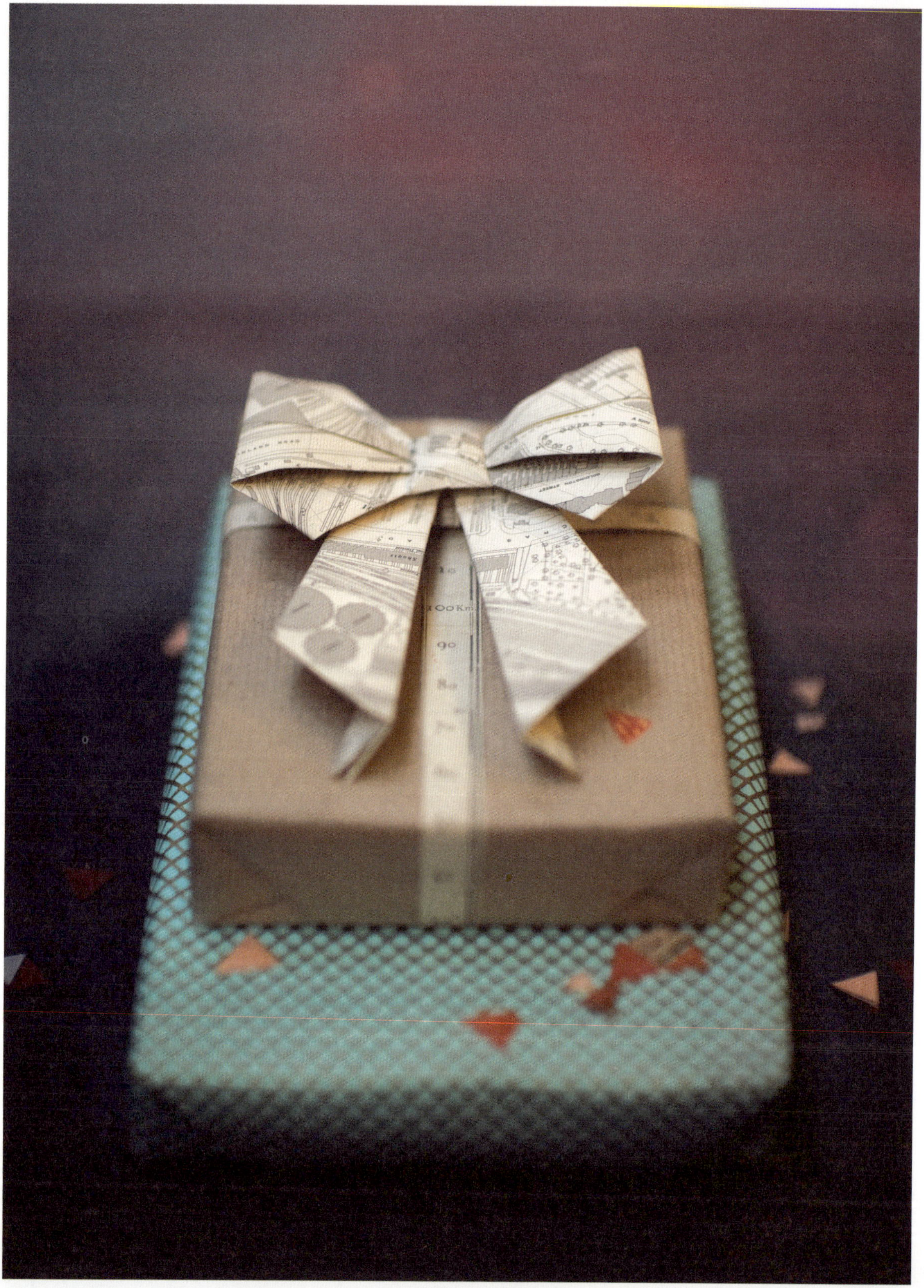

3

O·R·I·G·A·M·I B·O·W

m 30

£ 5 ↓

× ORIGAMI IS THE TRADITIONAL JAPANESE ART OF PAPER FOLDING. THE GOAL IS TO TAKE A FLAT SHEET OF PAPER AND TRANSFORM IT INTO A 3D SCULPTURE. IN ITS PUREST FORM, EVEN CUTS TO THE PAPER ARE OFF-LIMITS. THE SIMPLICITY OF THIS CONCEPT IS EXTREMELY ELEGANT AND ILLUSTRATES THE VALUE OF RULES IN CREATIVE THINKING. CONTRARY TO EXPECTATIONS, RULES ARE IN FACT AN IMPORTANT COMPONENT OF ANY CREATIVE GOAL. THE TIGHTER THE BRIEF, THE MORE CREATIVE YOU ARE FORCED TO BE.

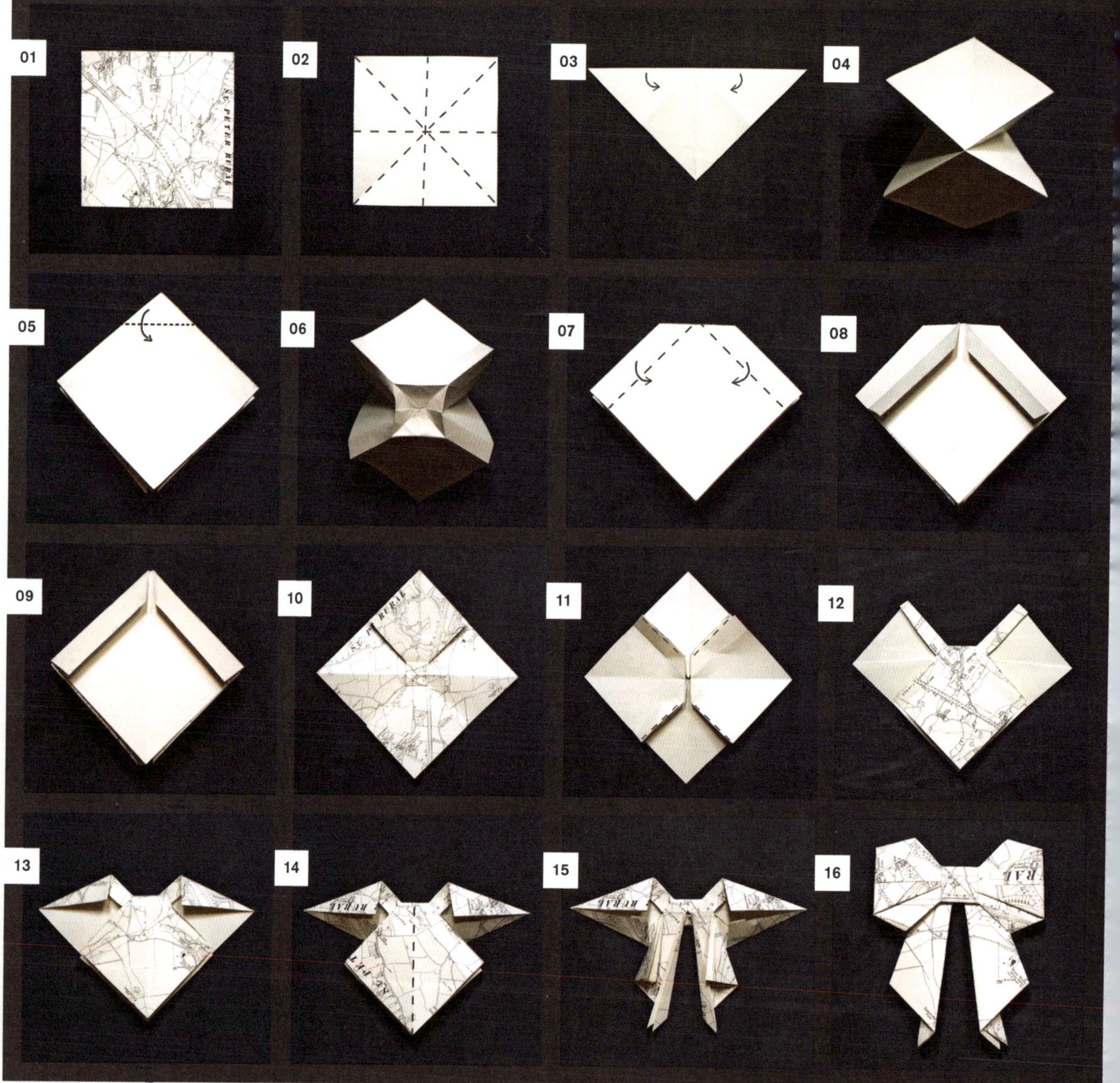
01
02
03
04
05
06
07
08
09
10
11
12
13
14
15
16

If you don't like what you've made just screw it up and start over

WHAT YOU NEED

- An old map
- Scissors

1. Cut a small part of your map into a perfect square of 15 x 15cm (6 x 6in).

2. Fold the square in half and use your fingertips to score the folded edge. Open it out and fold the square in half in the other direction. Open the square again and fold diagonally, then again on the other diagonal to form a triangle.

3. With the paper still folded in a triangle shape and the long side of the triangle at the top, hold the triangle at its bottom point and gently push the upper right-hand side of the triangle towards the bottom tip held in your left hand. Repeat on the left-hand side. The folds you have made in the paper will enable you to do this.

4. Now flatten your folded paper, tucking the upper parts of the original triangle inside the bottom parts of the triangle to form a diamond.

5. With the open ends at the bottom, fold the top of the diamond downwards by 1.5cm (⅔in) and score the fold with your fingertips. Repeat, folding the top of the diamond in the other direction.

6. Open out the diamond and score along each of the lines that forms the central square using your fingertips.

7. With the central square at the top, push two of its edges inwards so that the top of the diamond becomes inverted leaving a flattened top.

8. Now fold the top right edge in, scoring with your fingertips. Repeat on the left-hand side.

9. Turn the diamond over and do the same on the other side.

10. Next, carefully open out the square of paper by lifting the folded leaves upwards. Snip along the four folds that run inwards towards the centre of the square, as shown in image 10.

11. Turn the square over and flatten the central square – this will form the centre of the bow.

12. Turn the square over again and fold the top leaf down.

13. Take the right-hand leaf and fold the top edge in to the middle to create a point. Repeat on the bottom edge. Do the same for the left-hand leaf.

14. Now snip in half the remaining two leaves that are pointing down.

15. Take the right-hand tail and fold both sides inwards to give the tail shape. Now repeat on the left-hand tail.

16. Finally, turn the bow over and tuck each of the side points into the central square. *Et voilà* – you have a bow!

4

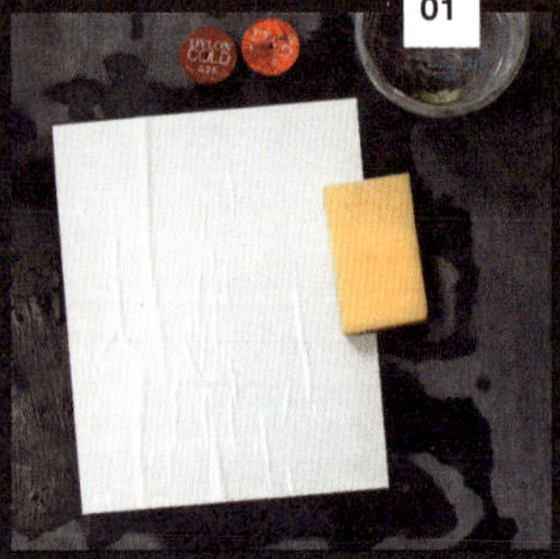

01

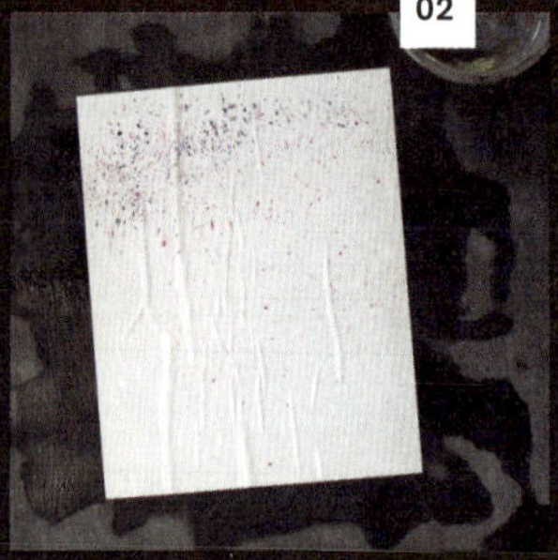

02

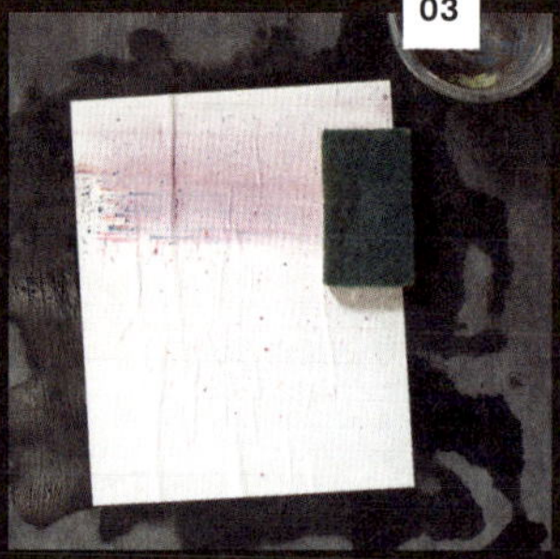

03

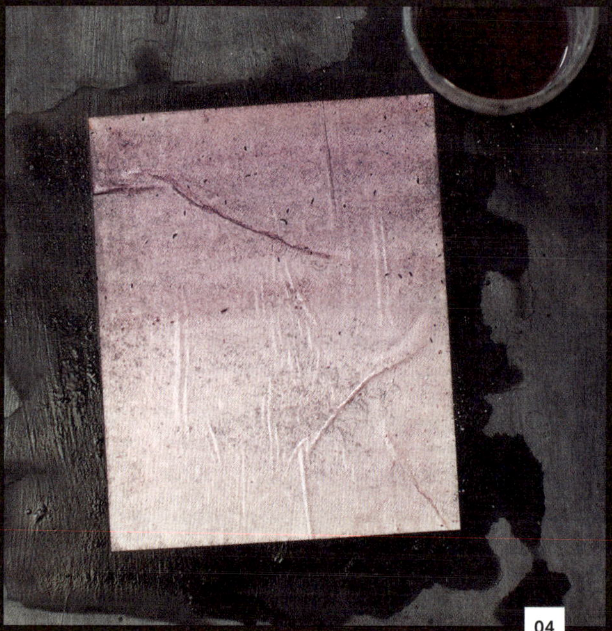

04

WHAT YOU NEED

- A few sheets of cartridge paper
- Sachets of Dylon dye; we used Olive Green, Burlesque Red, Powder Pink and Yellow
- Grey acrylic paint
- Plastic pot
- Sponge
- Plastic tablecloth or newspaper
- Rubber gloves
- Plastic apron
- Hairdryer

H·A·N·D-D·Y·E·D P·A·P·E·R

× CREATE A COLLECTION OF PRETTY PAPERS WITH JUST A HANDFUL OF INEXPENSIVE INGREDIENTS AND AN HOUR OR TWO OF YOUR TIME. EXPERIMENT WITH BRIGHT HUES AND MUTED TONES TO CREATE AN EYE-CATCHING ASSORTMENT OF SHADES THAT CAN BE USED AS THE MAIN MATERIAL FOR MANY OF THE PROJECTS THAT FOLLOW IN THIS BOOK.

1. Take a sheet of cartridge paper and lay it on a plastic tablecloth or some newspaper. Make sure you are wearing the plastic apron and some rubber gloves (otherwise the dye will stain your clothes and hands) and then fill your plastic pot with some warm water. Use the sponge to sweep water over the surface of the paper sheet.

2. Sprinkle a tiny bit of the darker dye straight across the upper third of the paper sheet, and then use the sponge to sweep the colour down the page all the way to the bottom. The colour on the bottom third of the paper should be very faint so as to create a faded effect.

3. Wash the sponge and then sprinkle a little of the lighter dye across the bottom third of the paper sheet. This time use the sponge to sweep the dye upwards towards the darker dye, blending the two colours as you go. If your preference is for slightly muted tones, try adding a small amount of grey acrylic paint directly to the paper to dull the colours. Mixing the acrylic paint in with the dye also helps to create a textured effect on the paper.

4. Repeat the same process on the other sheets of paper, this time making sure to use different proportions and mixes of the various colours to give you a wide range of coloured papers. Leave the sheets to dry, and then repeat the process on the back of the paper. When both sides are dry the paper is ready to use. Feel free to use a hairdryer to speed up the drying process.

e | h 1-2 | £ 10

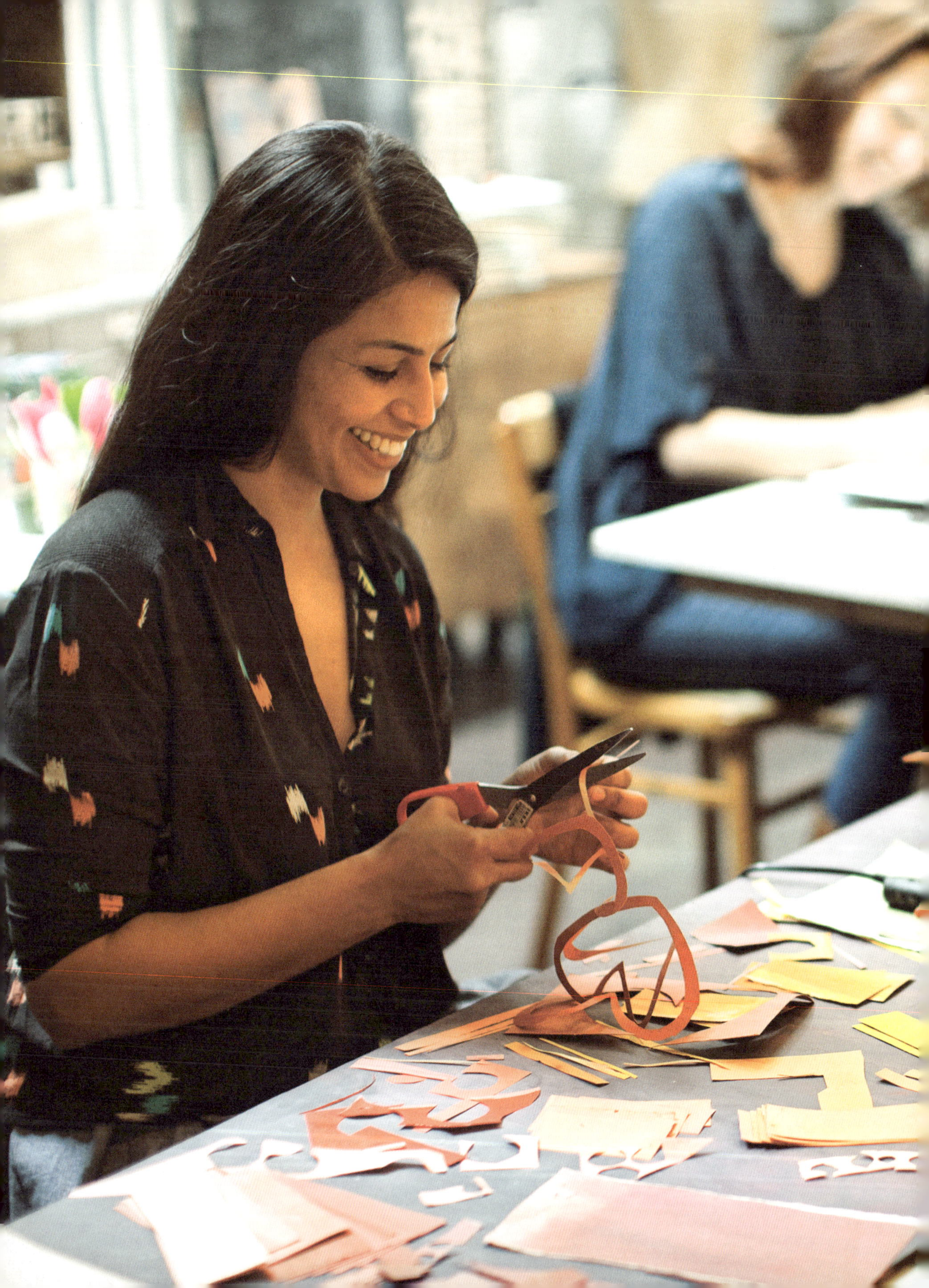

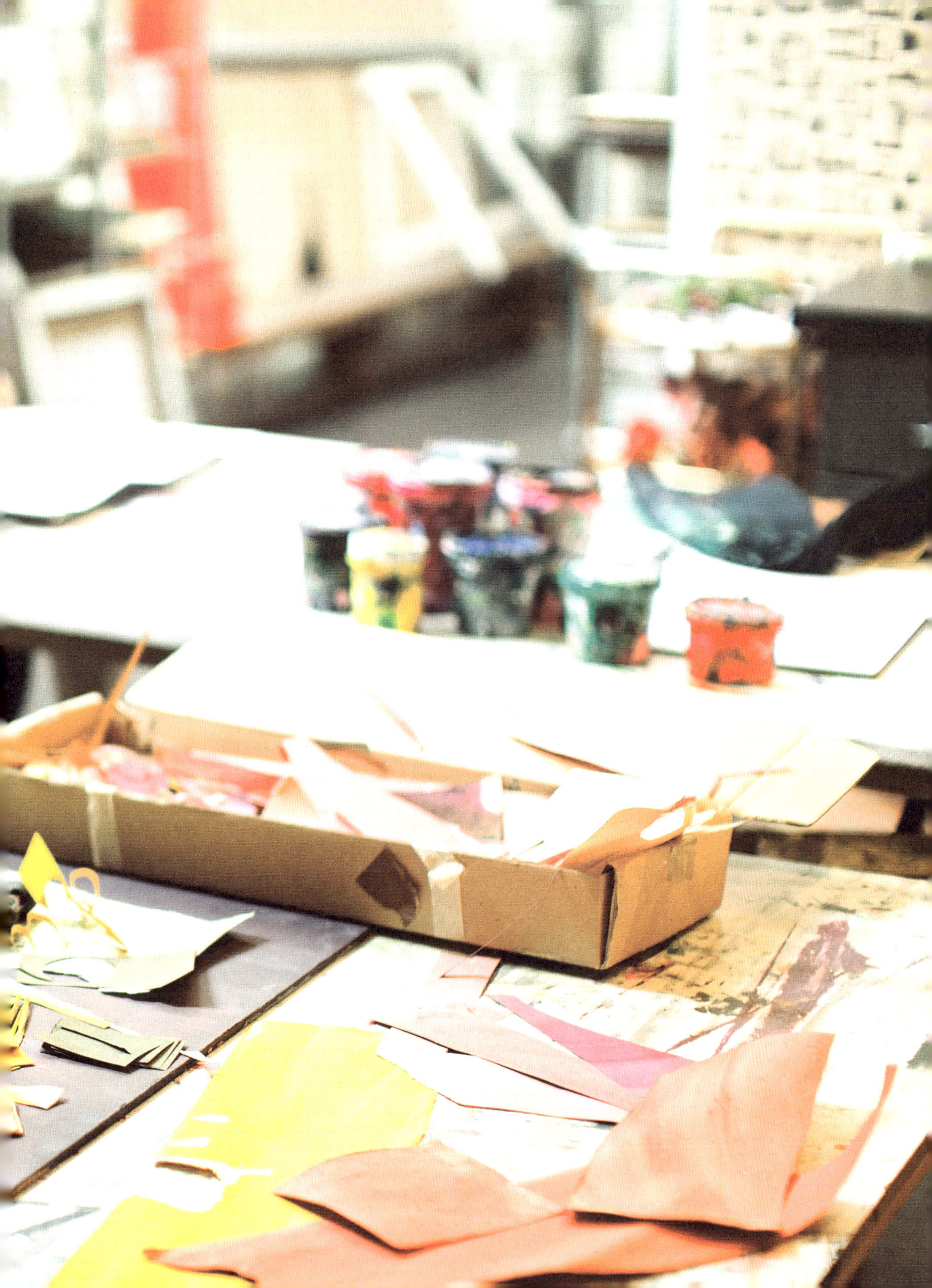

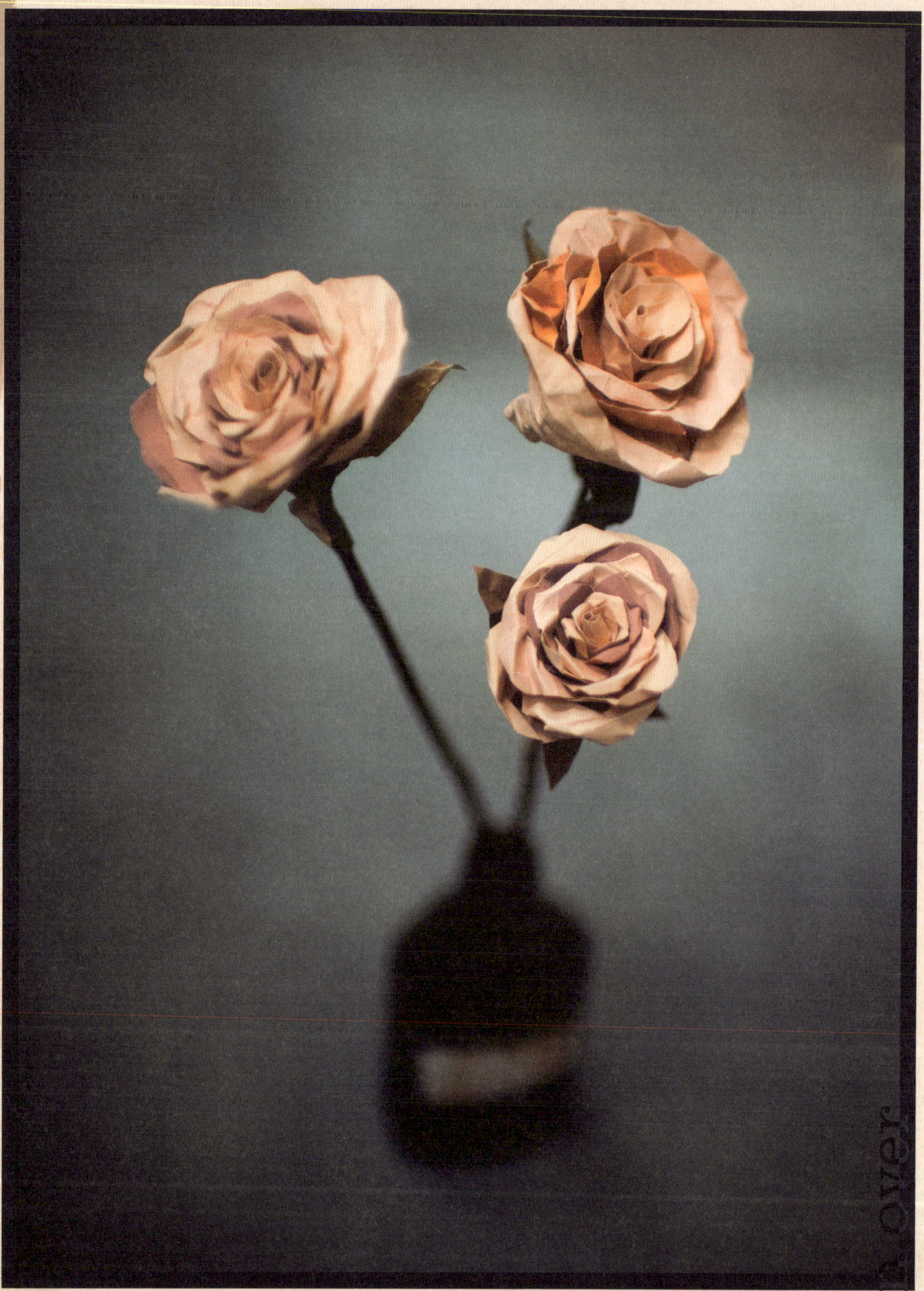

urn over

5

P·A·P·E·R R·O·S·E

× PAPER ROSES ARE THE PERFECT CENTRE PIECE FOR ANY TABLE SETTING. NOT ONLY DO THEY LOOK STUNNING IN A VASE, THEY ARE SURPRISINGLY SIMPLE TO MAKE. SO WHETHER YOU WANT TO BRING A FLORAL FLOURISH TO YOUR HOME OR ADD A TOUCH OF ROMANCE, TRY A PAPER ROSE, IT WILL SMELL JUST AS SWEET.

new leaf,
urn over a
ew leaf

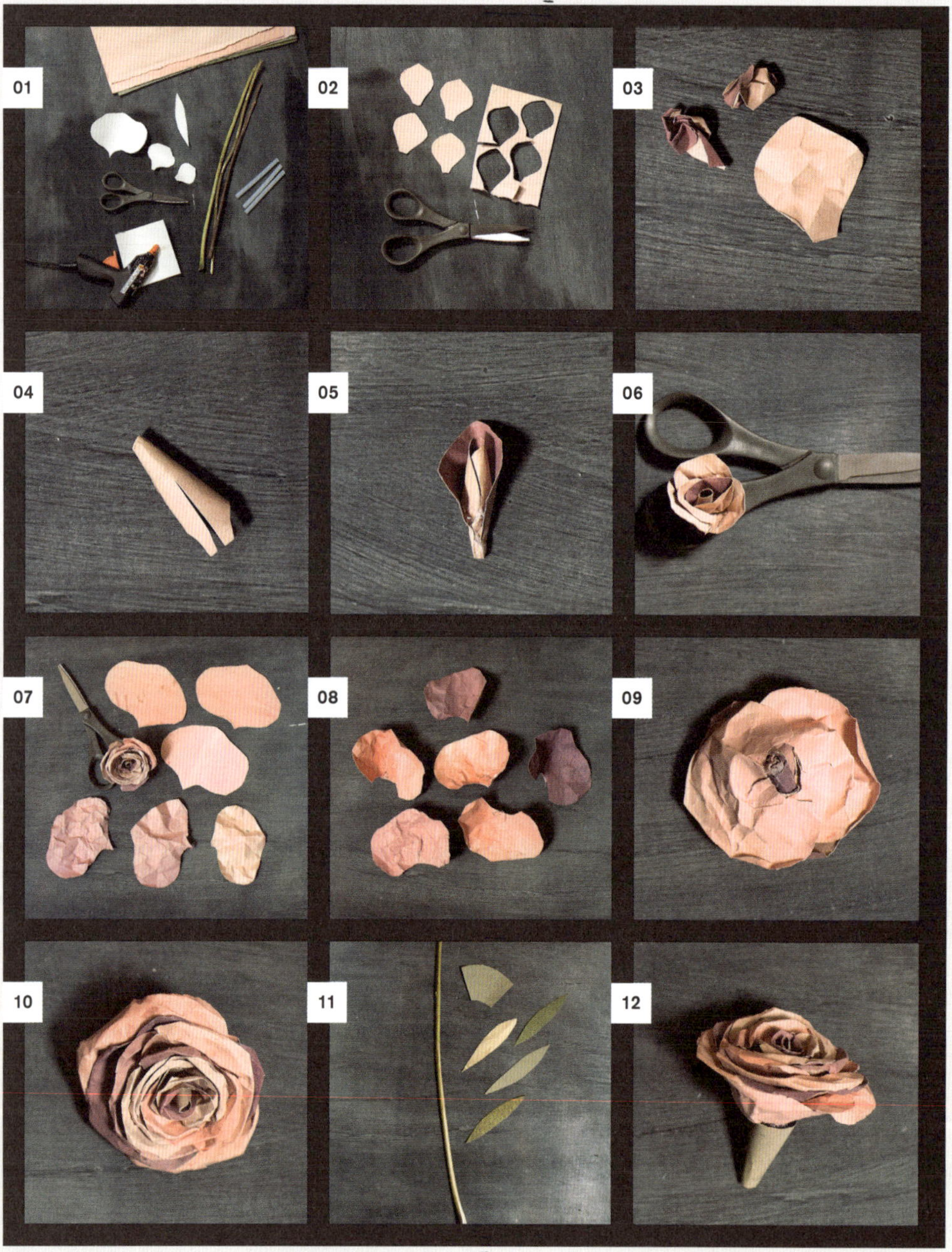
01
02
03
04
05
06
07
08
09
10
11
12

The devil is in the detail, so have a real rose to hand to check progress as you go

WHAT YOU NEED

- A few sheets of hand-dyed paper (see page 26)
- Glue gun and glue sticks
- Scissors
- 3 dried rose stems

1. Switch your glue gun on and leave it to heat up on a piece of paper to catch any leaking glue. Cut out three petal templates as shown in image 01.

2. Starting with the smallest template, cut out four petals from one of the lightest coloured sheets of hand-dyed paper.

3. Scrunch each petal into a little ball to break down the starch in the paper, and then smooth them out again. The petals will now be easier to shape.

4. Take the first petal and hold it at the narrow end. Roll the top edges of the petal to form a point and secure with a tiny dab of glue from the glue gun. Turn the petal over and snip up the back with the scissors. Then fold one side of the cut over the other to pinch the petal in at the bottom. Again, secure with a dab of glue.

5. Take a second petal and squeeze a very thin line of glue across the bottom of it. Stick the second petal to the pinched-in end of the first petal, making sure to tease and sculpt the petals as you work. Repeat with the next two petals, overlapping one quarter of each new petal with the petal before it. Every now and then make sure you use a petal that is a slightly different colour. This will help to give your rose a more realistic quality.

6. Using the medium-sized petal template, repeat the same process with six more petals.

7. Take the largest template and cut out six large petals. This time make all the petals a slightly different shape. We also suggest you make each of the six petals slightly bigger than the last. As before, don't forget to scrunch up and unroll each petal before adding them to the rose.

8. Hold the first of the large petals with the point between your fingers. Using your thumb and forefinger, ease the right-hand side of the petal over the left-hand side to form a small pleat in the centre of the petal. Stick the pleat down with glue from the glue gun. The aim of the pleat is to add a slight curve to the petal. Next, cut off the tip of the petal so that the bottom of the petal forms a neat curve.

9. This time when you attach the petals, stick them slightly higher up the rose leaving the central part of the rose bud sticking out a little at the back.

10. Once all of the petals have been attached, spend a little time arranging and shaping the edges of the petals to make the rose look as realistic as possible.

11. Now take a small piece of green paper and cut out four leaves and an eighth of a circle to make a cone base. Remember to scrunch up the leaves and smooth them out again.

12. Attach the cone base to the rose, leaving a hole for the stem to slip into. Squeeze some glue into the hole, and then attach the stem. Finally, arrange the leaves and stick them securely to the stem. Now repeat as many times as you like to make an entire bunch of roses.

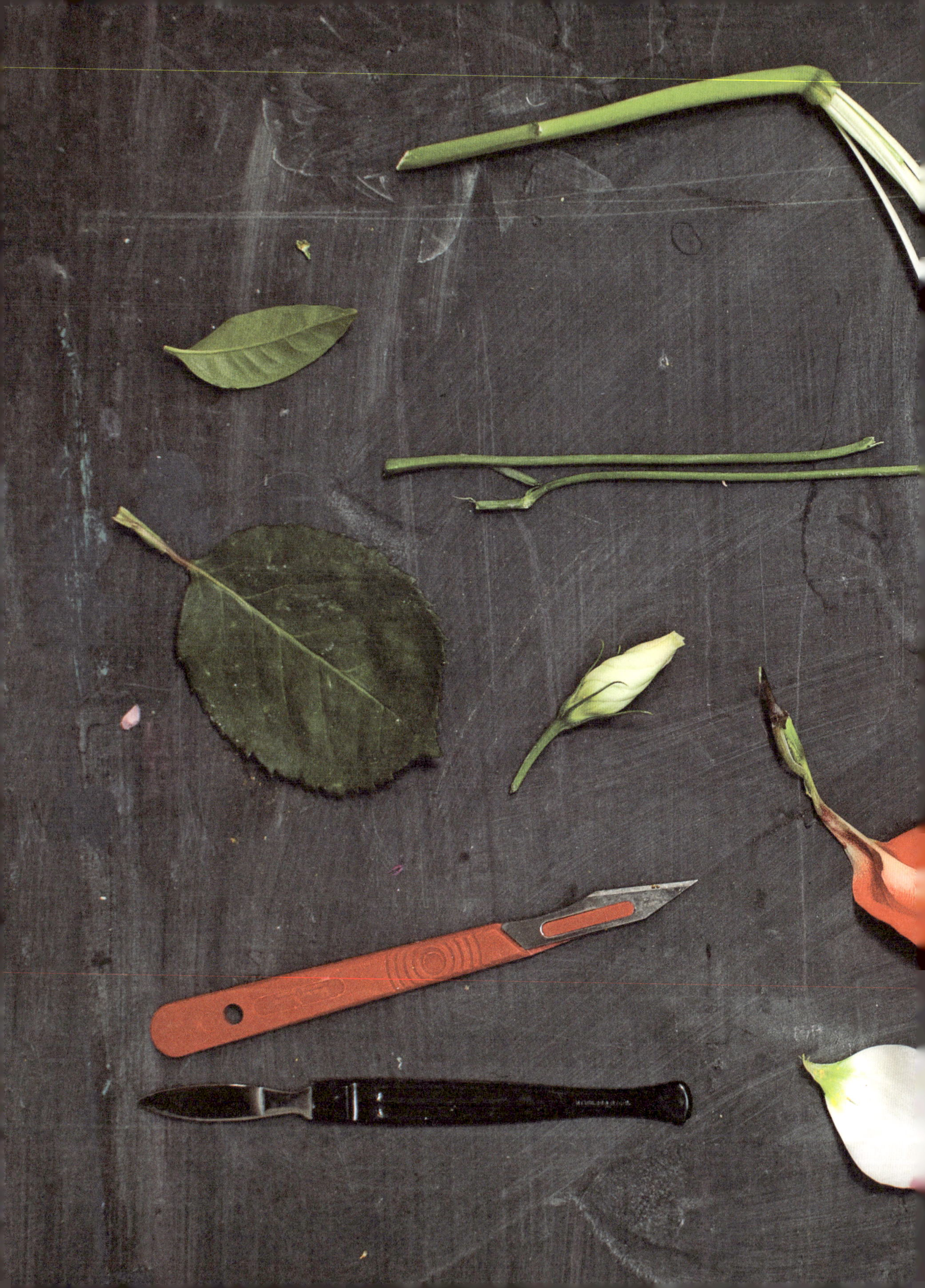

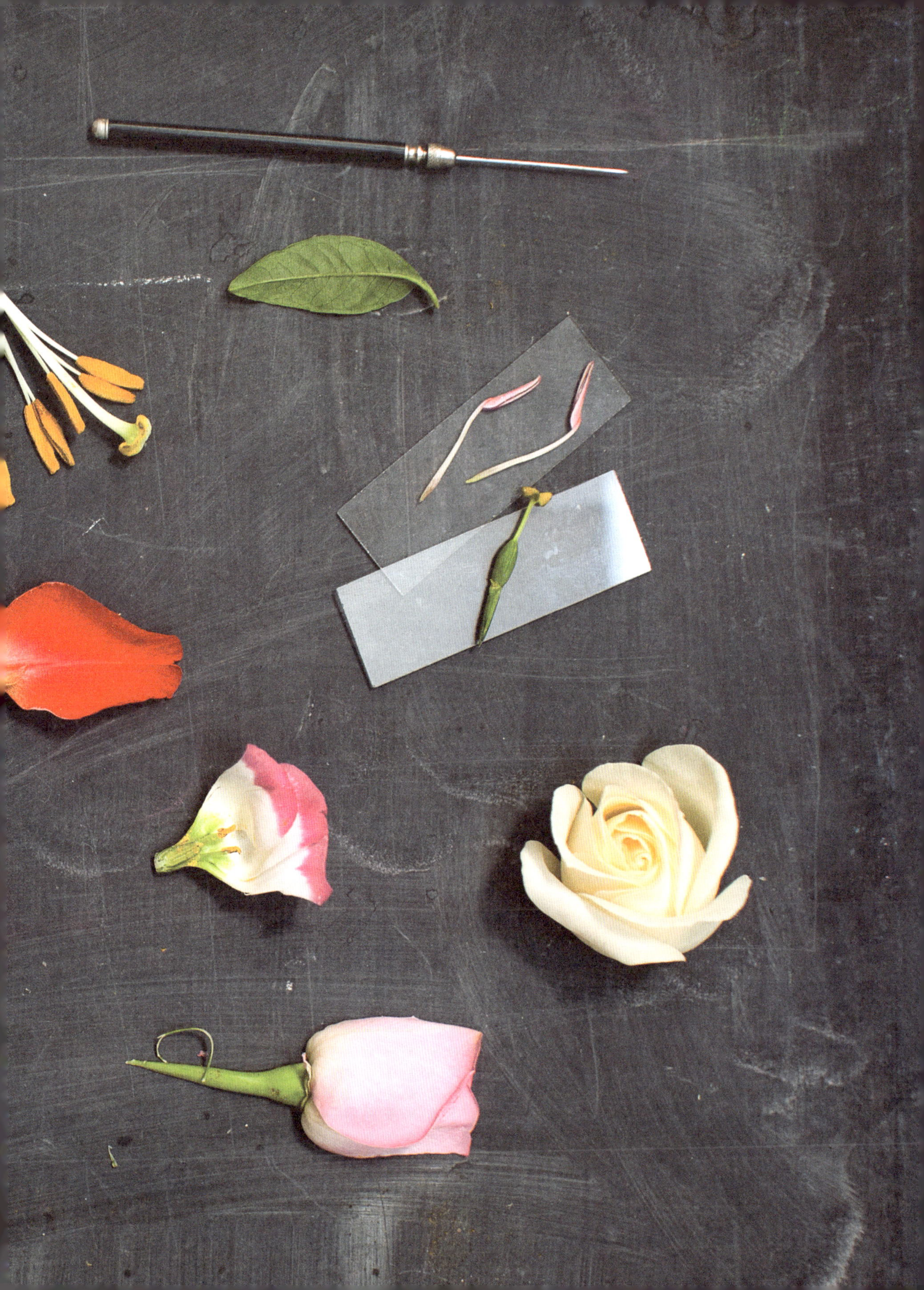

6

WHAT YOU NEED

- A few sheets of hand-dyed paper (see page 26)
- An old map or any other type of paper that will look beautiful as an envelope (sheet music, book pages)
- Glue
- Washi tape
- Recycled envelope

P·A·P·E·R E·N·V·E·L·O·P·E·S

× IF YOU'D SOONER SEND A LOVINGLY WRITTEN LETTER THAN AN INSTANT EMAIL, THEN A HANDMADE ENVELOPE DELIVERED TO THE DOORSTEP IS JUST THE THING.

1. Take a used envelope out of the recycling bin and open each of its edges out by using a letter opener or knife to reveal its original net shape. In most cases you should end up with something that looks like four triangles radiating out from a square or rectangle – or a stack of three rectangles with a triangle at the top and small wings on either side.

2. Using the opened-out envelope as a template, cut out a new net shape from one of your pieces of coloured paper or maps. Fold the envelope together and fix it all in place with a few dabs of glue.

3. Print out the name and address of the recipient in a typewriter font on the computer (or better still on a real typewriter) and use Washi tape to decorate it. Repeat the process with other types of envelope to give you a variety of shapes and sizes.

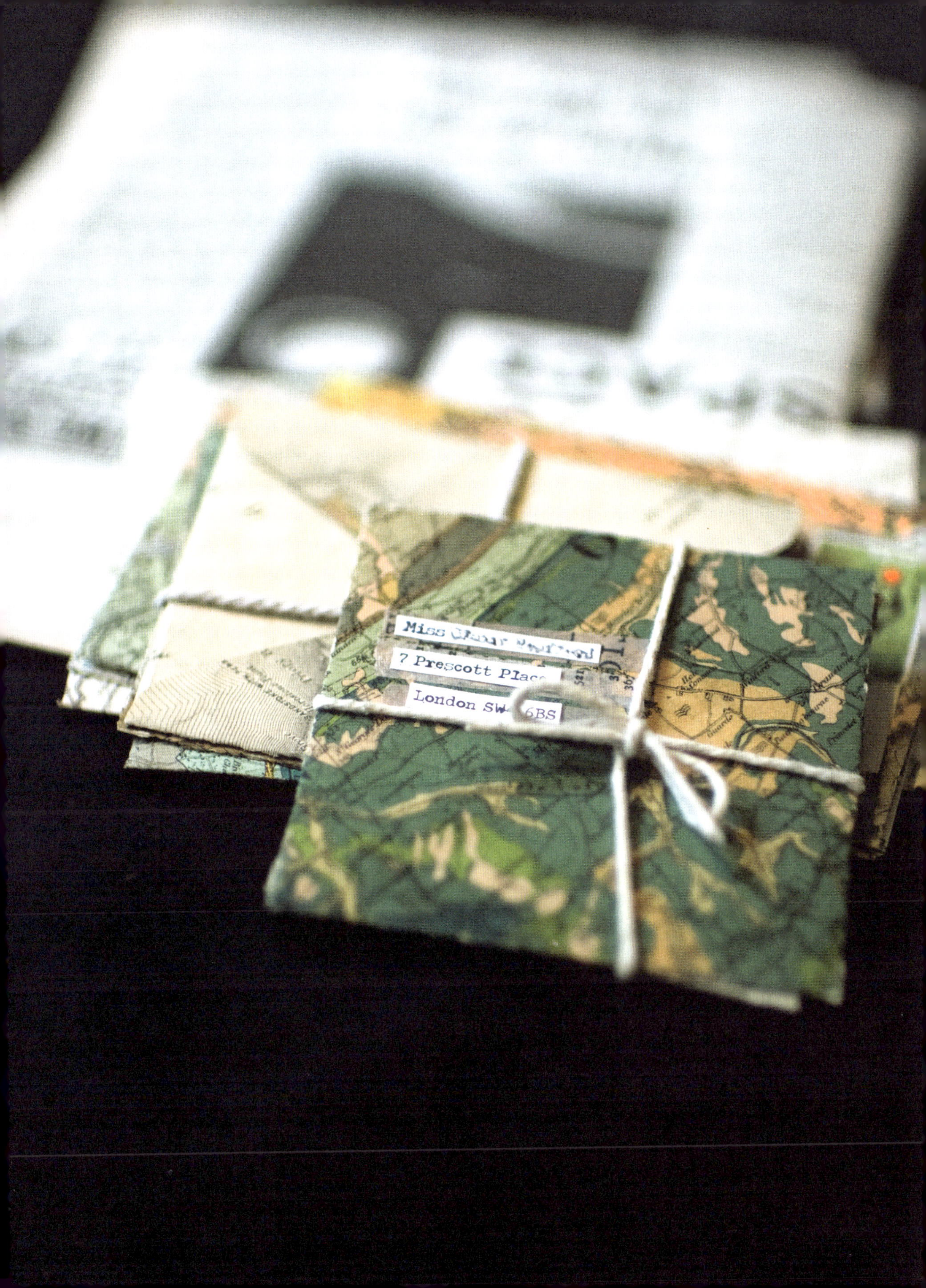
Miss
7 Prescott Plac
London SW

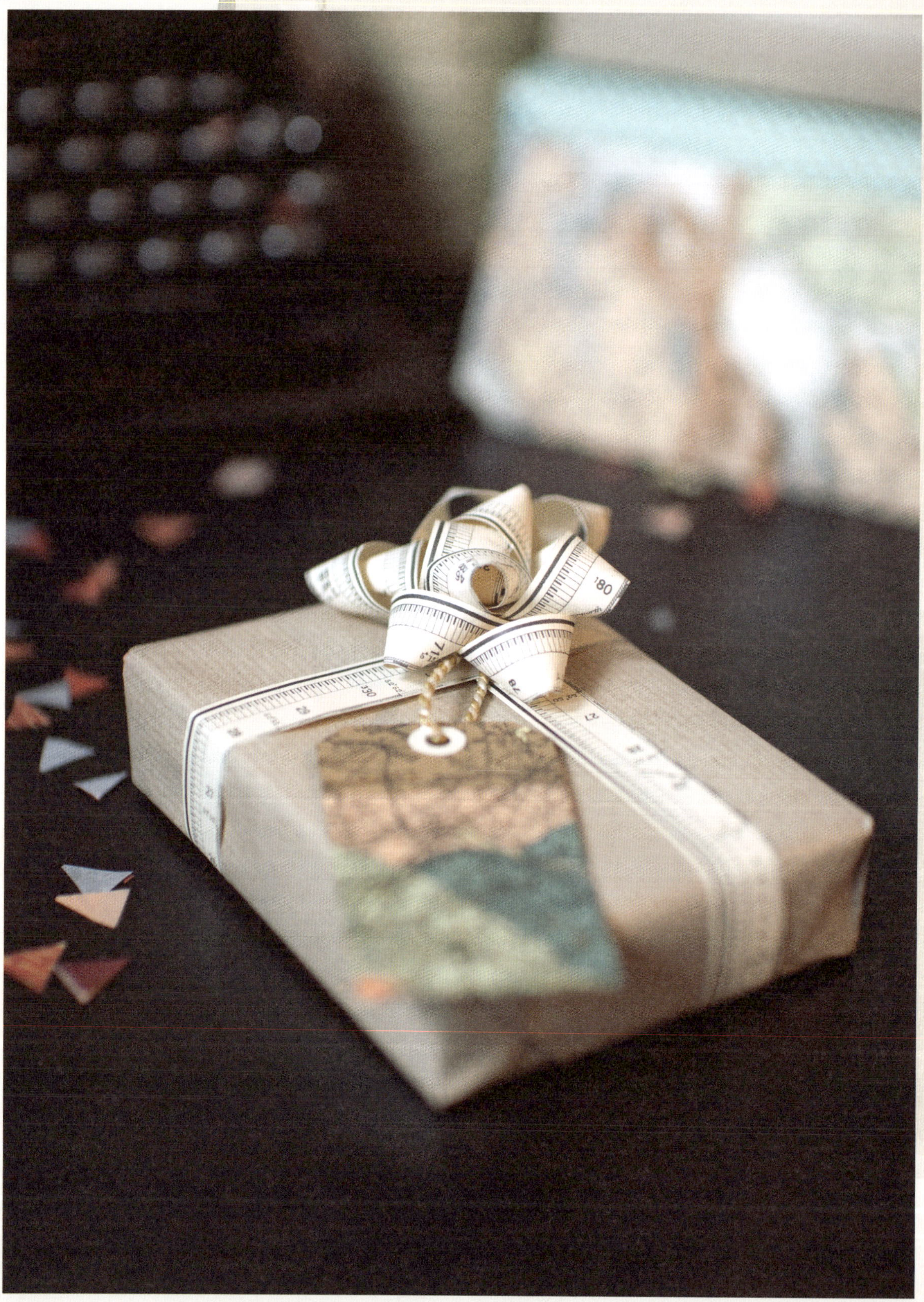

S·T·A·R B·O·W 7

39

× PUT A CONTEMPORARY TWIST ON BROWN PAPER PACKAGES TIED UP WITH STRING AS YOU CURL, LOOP AND STICK YOUR WAY TO PERFECTLY WRAPPED PRESENTS.

e

m 15

£ 5 ↓

WHAT YOU NEED

- An old map
- Brown paper
- Scissors
- Glue gun and glue sticks or needle and thread

A gift for wrapp
gift for wrappin
for wrapping

WRAP YOUR GIFT

1. Begin by wrapping your gift in brown paper. If it's an unusual shape put it in a box before you wrap – you'll get a neater edge when you fold the paper in at the corners.

2. Take an old map and cut off the black and white edges around the outside where the coordinates are printed. Cut these pieces into neat strips to use as ribbons.

3. Wrap one of the ribbons you've just made horizontally around the gift and secure it with a dab of glue. Then do the same vertically with a second strip to form a pretty cross. The cross does not need to be centred.

MAKE YOUR BOW

1. Take the remaining pieces of paper ribbon and cut them into three ribbons of three lengths: approximately 15cm (6in), 20cm (8in) and 25cm (10in) long, as shown in image 01.

2. Take the longest strip and hold one end between the thumb and forefinger of your left hand, plain side up. With your right hand take hold of the loose end of the paper and twist it to form your first loop. Repeat so that you have two loops. Secure the loops with a dab of glue from the glue gun, as shown in image 02.

3. Now make and secure one more loop so that you have a three-loop triangle, as shown in image 03.

4. Make two more three-loop triangles from the remaining two lengths of paper ribbon

5. Stick the three triangles together – one on top of the other in descending size – with a dab of glue from the glue gun. Alternatively, you could stitch them together with a needle and thread and secure with a knot on the back of the bow, as shown in images 04, 05 and 06.

6. With another dab of glue, attach the bow to the centre of the paper ribbon cross on the gift – and you're done.

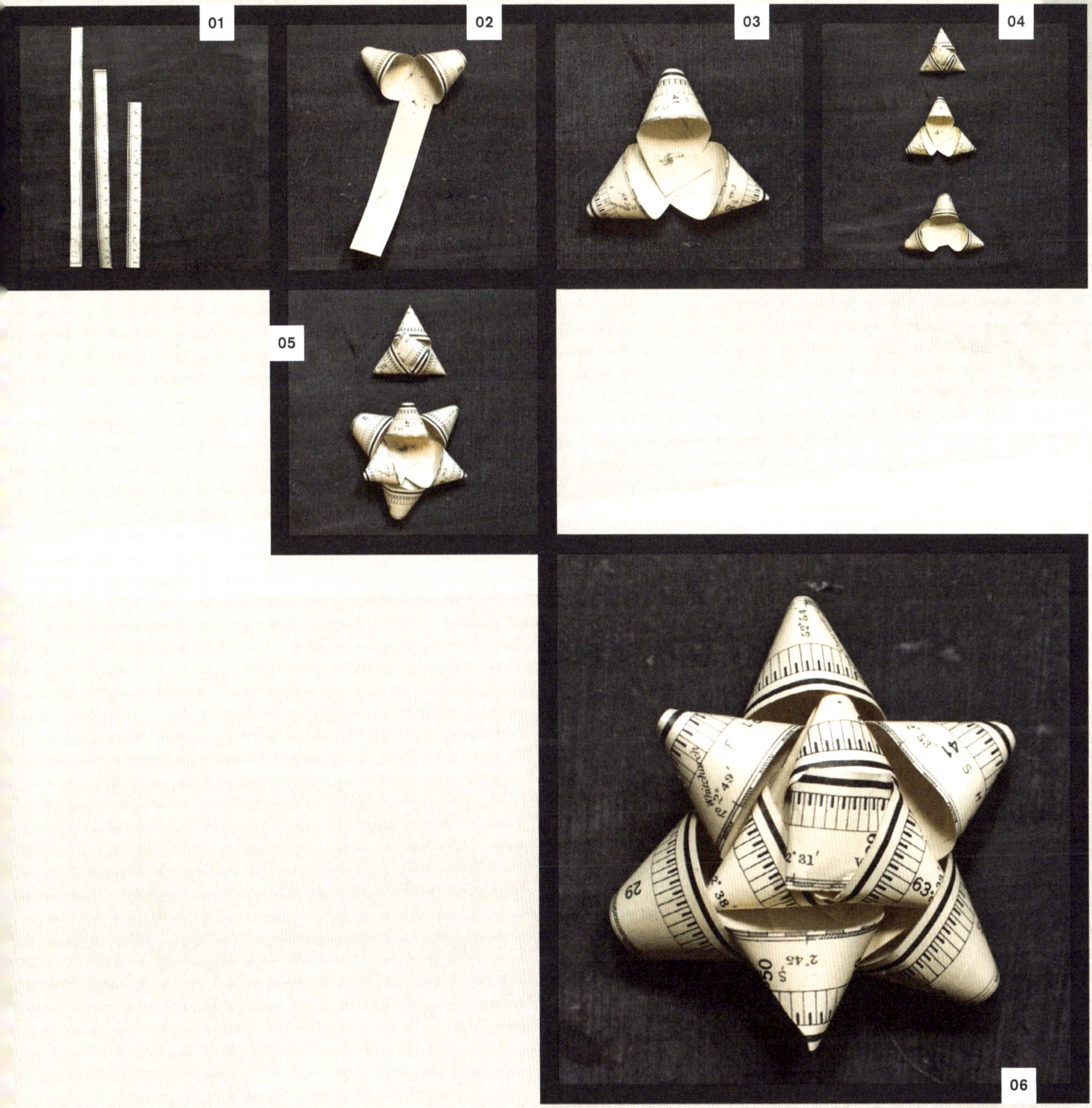
01
02
03
04
05
06

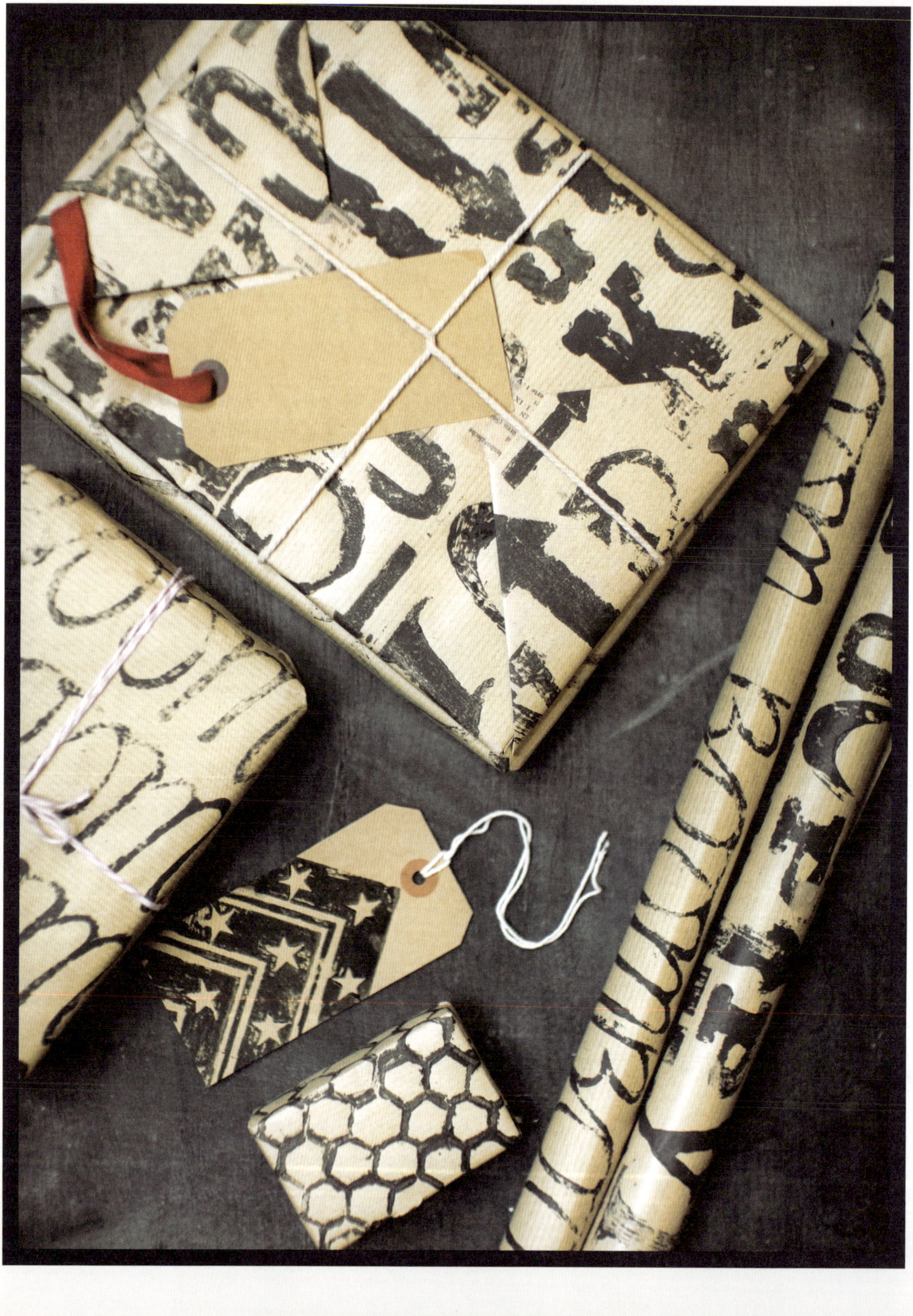

8

W·R·A·P·P·I·N·G P·A·P·E·R

WHAT YOU NEED

- Vintage printing blocks
- Roll of brown paper
- Acrylic paint
- Plastic pot
- Plastic tray
- Stippling brush
- Printing roller
- Scissors

× PRINT YOUR OWN WRAPPING PAPER USING VINTAGE PRINTING BLOCKS. BEGIN BY SPENDING A LITTLE TIME COLLECTING A SMALL SELECTION OF BLOCKS FROM LOCAL ANTIQUES MARKETS OR BRIC-A-BRAC SHOPS, AND DON'T FORGET THERE'S ALWAYS EBAY. YOU CAN EXPECT TO PAY AROUND £3–£4 PER BLOCK – AND MAKING WRAPPING PAPER, GREETINGS CARDS AND TAGS IS A GREAT WAY TO PUT THEM TO USE. ALTERNATIVELY, MAKE YOUR OWN SIMPLE PRINTING BLOCKS BY FOLLOWING THE INSTRUCTIONS IN PROJECT 18 (SEE PAGE 86).

1. Take a roll of brown paper and cut it into a number of A4 (letter) size pieces. These are for use in the testing phase. Cut the remaining brown paper into large wrapping-paper size sheets.

2. Using a plastic pot, mix your acrylic paints into your chosen hue. An inky black with a hint of blue works particularly well on brown paper and grey works well on the lighter tones of tissue paper.

3. Using your A4 (letter) size test sheets, begin by inking up your blocks and testing the way they print on the paper. Some blocks will work best when the paint is applied with a stippling brush. Alternatively, if using a roller, put a small amount of paint into a plastic tray, and then use the roller to apply a thin layer of paint to the block.

4. Repeat the test prints a number of times until you discover the best way to get the block to print.

5. Once you are feeling confident with the printing process, begin experimenting with different ways of creating printed repeats. Aim to produce a pattern that pops once the repeat is established. You may find that you have to play around for quite a while until you get something you are happy with.

6. Repeat the testing process around five times so that you generate a number of different pattern options.

7. Finally, print up your chosen designs on the larger sheets of brown paper. Don't worry if the block slips while printing or you get the odd spot of paint exactly where you don't want it, these little imperfections are what will give your designs their character.

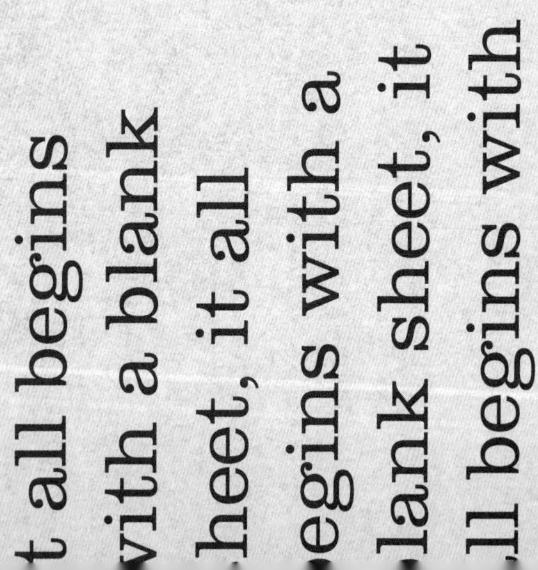

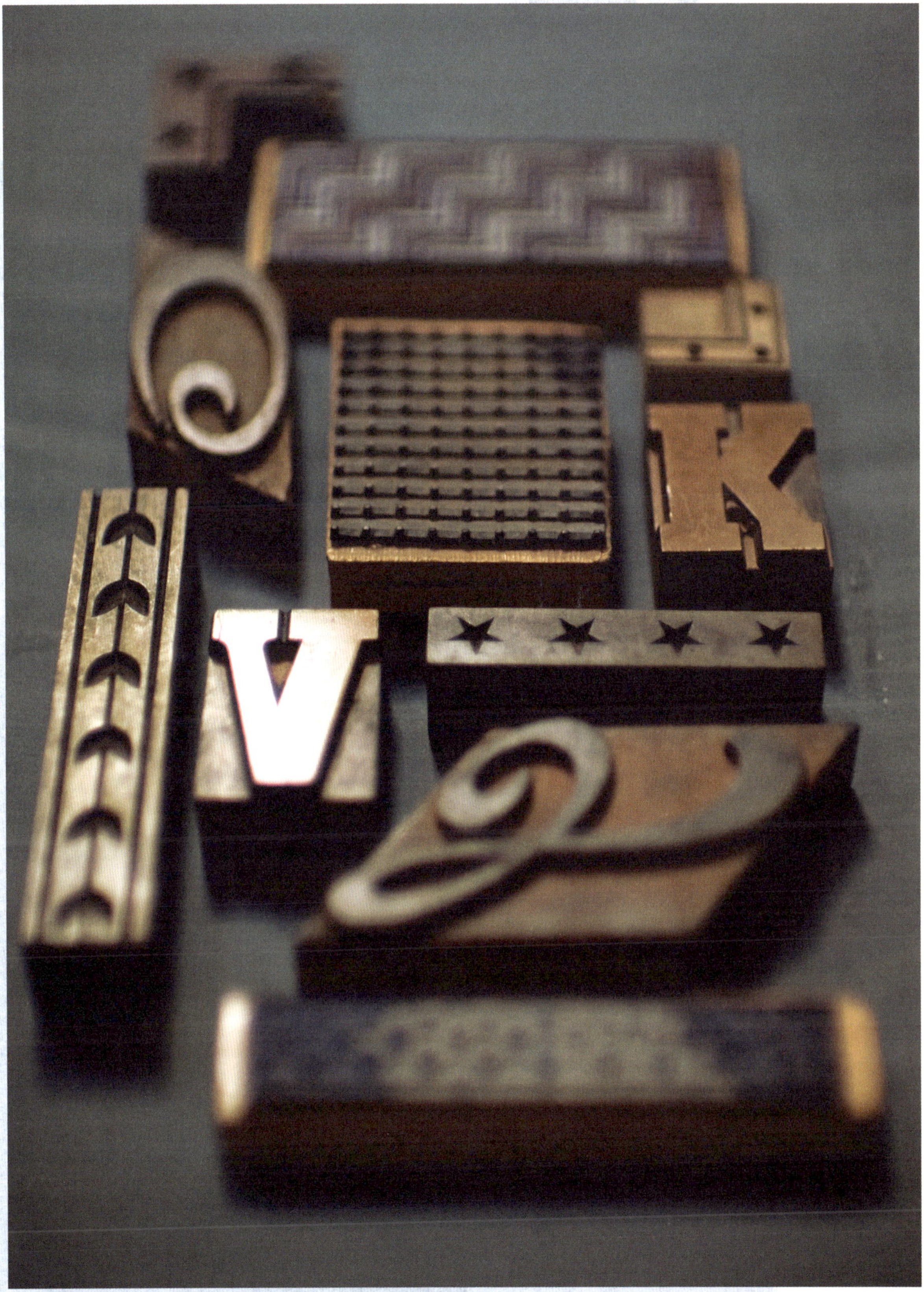

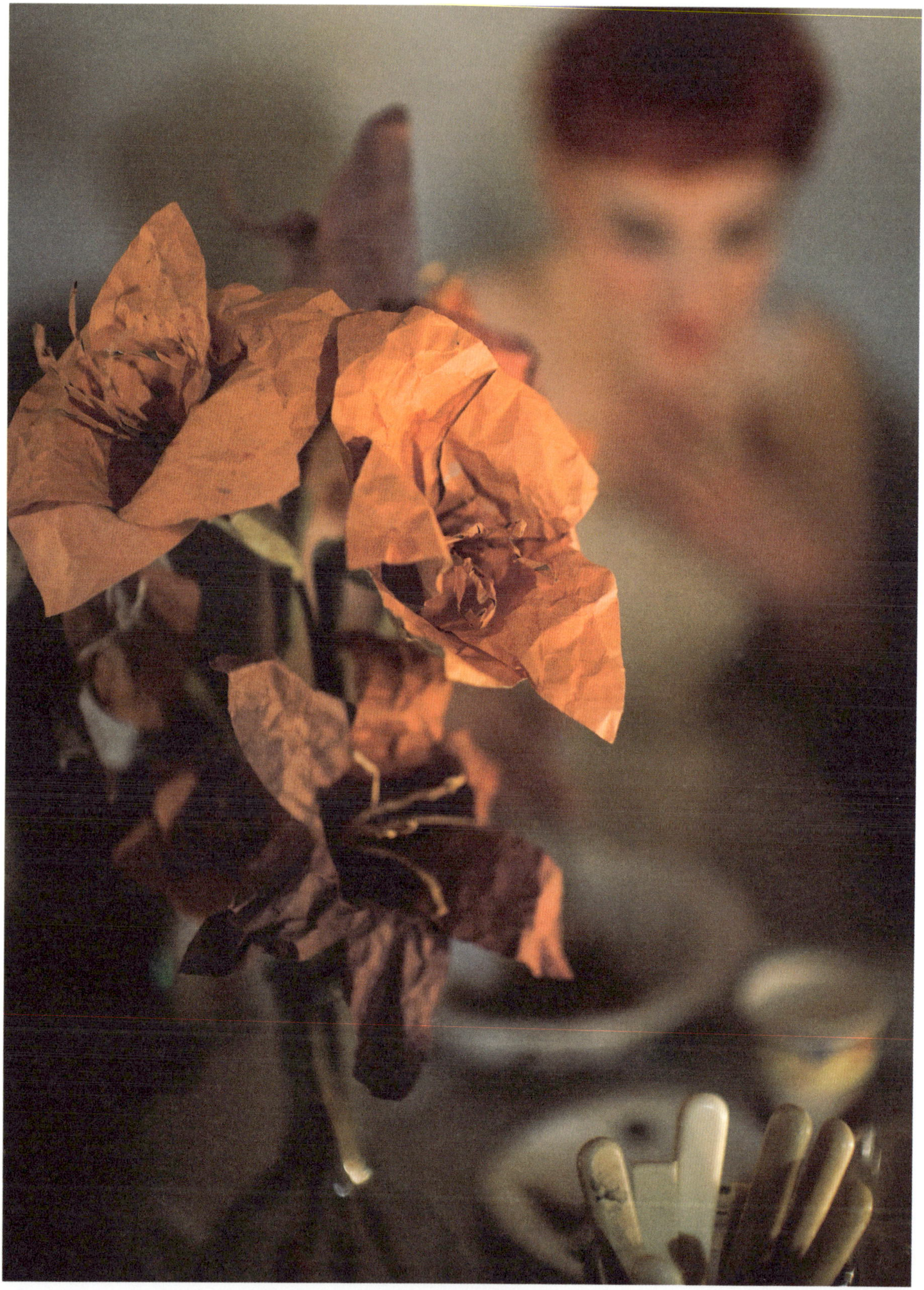

9

G·I·A·N·T L·I·L·I·E·S

WHAT YOU NEED

- A selection of hand-dyed paper (see page 26)
- A few dried flower stems
- Pencil
- Scissors
- Glue gun and glue sticks
- Sheet of plain paper
- Yellow and green cartridge paper

× THESE GIANT LILIES ARE PLAYFUL, EYE-CATCHING AND EASY TO MAKE – AND UNLIKE THEIR FRESH COUNTERPARTS, THEY LAST FOREVER. ONCE YOU'VE GOT THE HANG OF CONSTRUCTING THE FLOWERS, WHY NOT TRY DISSECTING OTHER VARIETIES TO EXPLORE THE WAY DIFFERENT PETALS ARE FORMED. THEN, WHEN YOU'RE READY, MOVE ON TO MAKING A MIXED STEM ARRANGEMENT – THE BIGGER THE BETTER!

m   h 5   £ 10↓

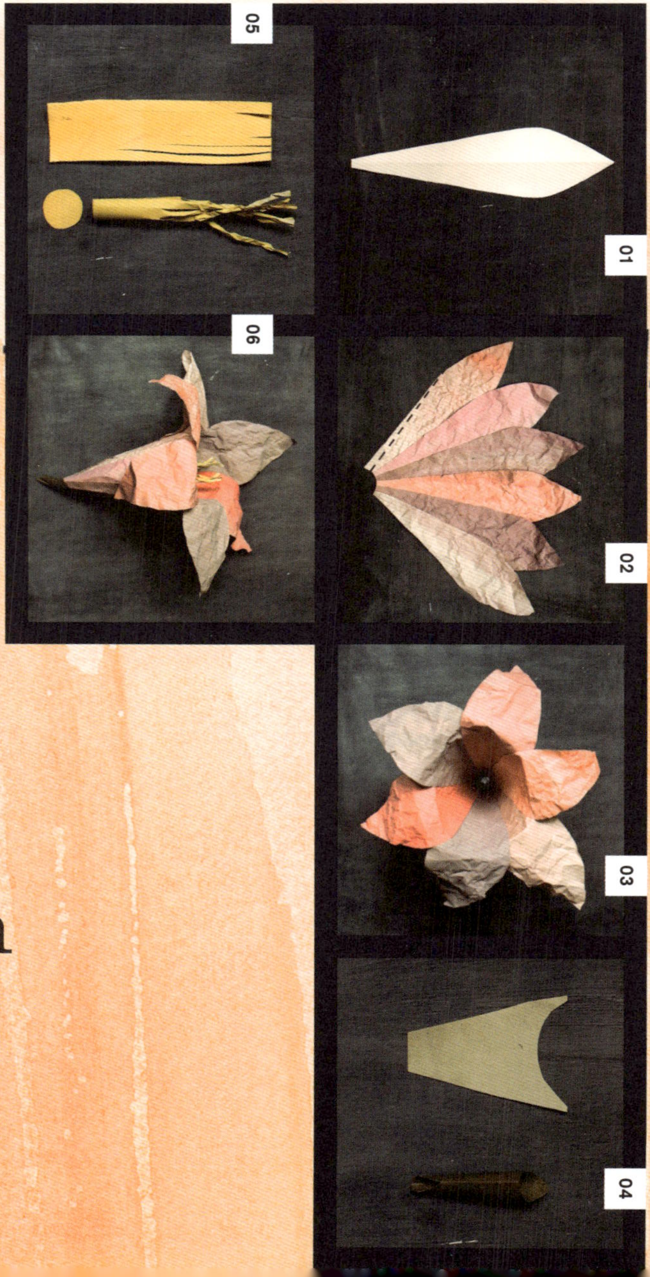

Try playing around with scale to create unusual or quirky designs

1. Switch your glue gun on and leave it to heat up on a piece of paper to catch any leaking glue. Cut out a lily petal template as shown in image 01. Use the template to cut out six petals, making sure to use a variety of colours in a range of subtle pinks and purples. As with the rose on page 30, once the petals are cut out, make sure you scrunch them up to break down the starch in the paper, and to give them a more organic look.

2. Take all six petals and overlay one petal onto another in turn to form a quarter circle. Stick the petals together with the glue gun, and then trim the bottom of the petals into a neat curve. At the same time, trim a little off the edges of the two outer petals, as shown in image 02.

3. Now curve the quarter circle of petals round so that the two sides meet with a narrower opening at the bottom of the petals and a broader opening at the top. Secure the join with a line of glue that runs from the bottom to the broadest part of the petals. You now have the main part of the lily complete.

4. Take a small piece of green cartridge paper and cut out the angled cone base. Roll the cone edges together and secure with a line of glue. Now attach the angled cone to the base of the flower using a large dab of glue. The head of the lily should sit at a slight angle.

5. To make the stamen, cut out a long rectangle of yellow cartridge paper, and then cut five slits running two thirds of the way down the length of the rectangle. Roll the rectangle into a cylinder and join the edges with a line of glue, then take each of the six strands and twist them into a more solid, 3D form. Finally, cut a circle of yellow paper and then glue the bottom of the cylinder to the circle before gluing the circle inside the centre of the flower.

6. Finish by attaching the lily to a dried flower stem, again using the glue gun. If necessary, reinforce the joint by wrapping it with additional layers of green paper and glue.

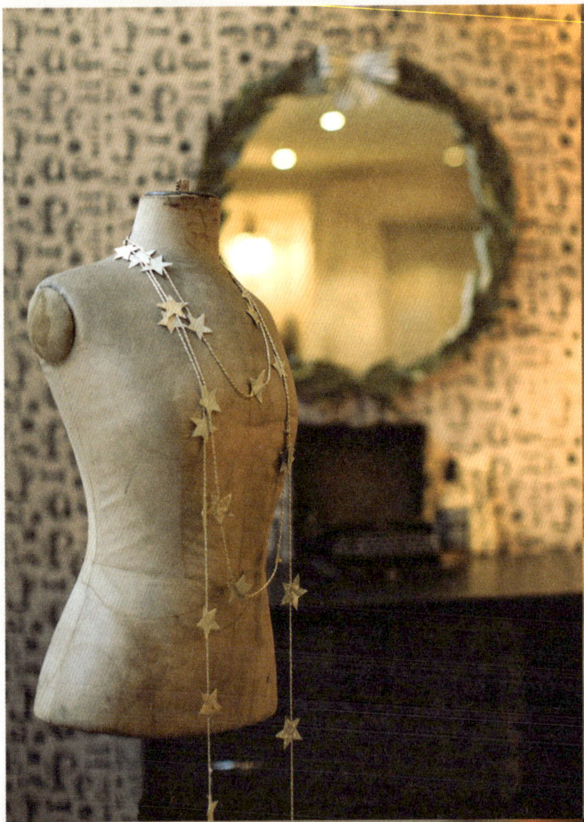
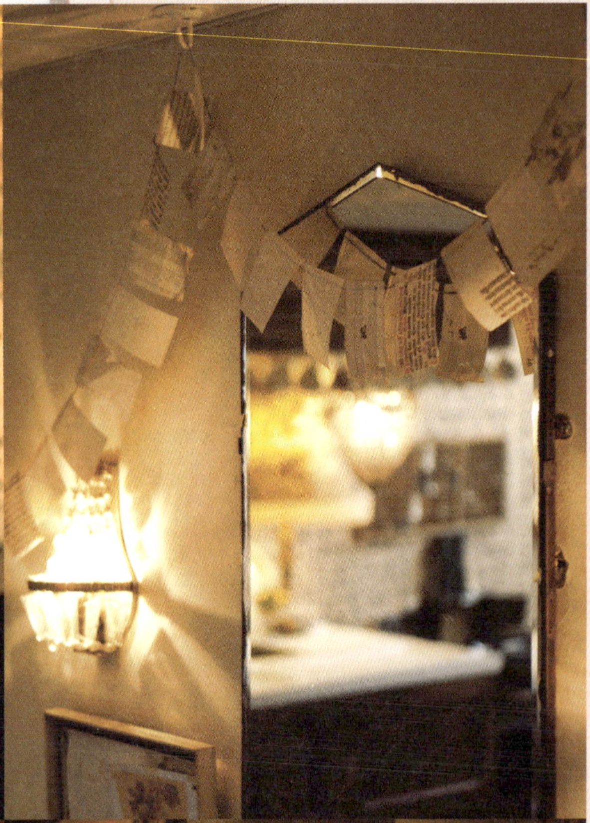
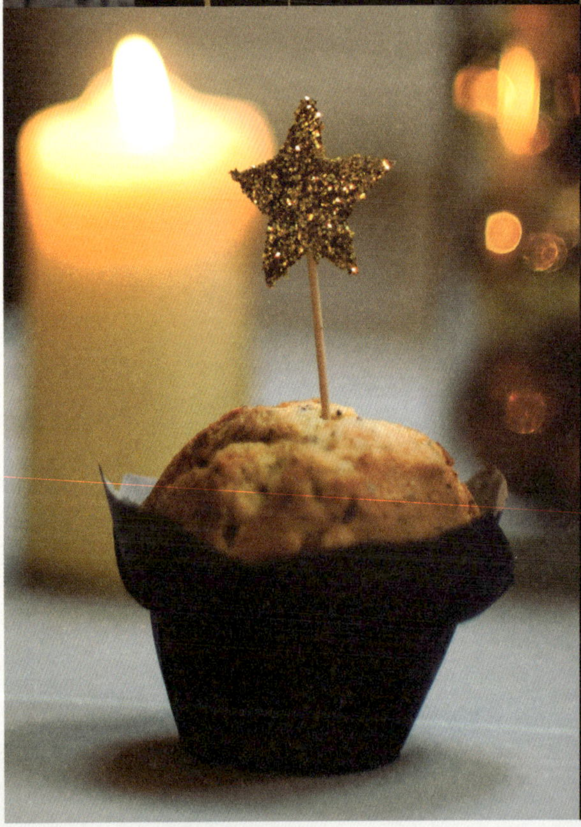
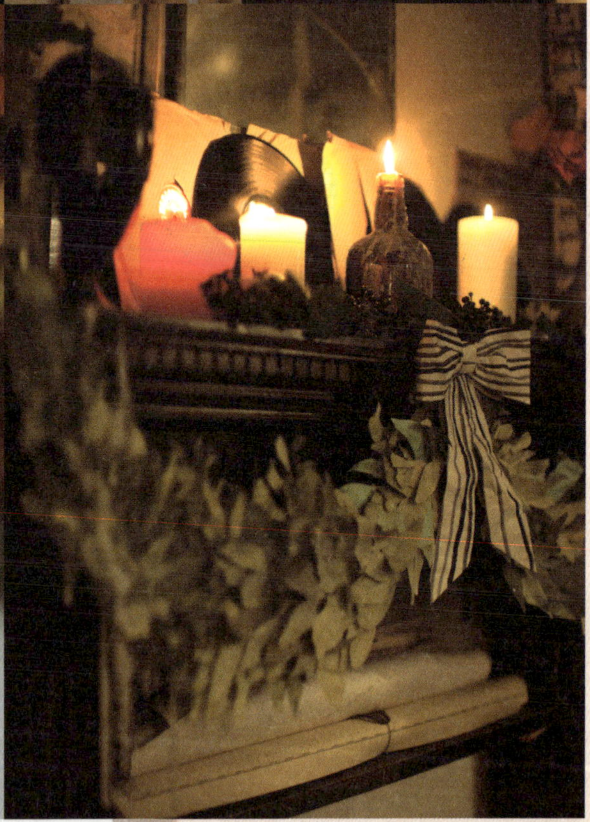

10

WHAT YOU NEED

- A selection of paper (old maps, sheet music, book pages)
- Cardboard
- Pencil
- Glue gun and glue sticks
- Scissors
- Cotton furnishing braid

P·A·P·E·R D·E·C·O·R·A·T·I·O·N·S

× THE FLEXIBILITY AND VERSATILITY OF PAPER MAKES IT THE IDEAL MATERIAL FOR MAKING DECORATIONS. FROM BUMPER VINTAGE-STYLE BUNTING TO ELEGANT SWAGS THAT FRAME A FIREPLACE – THERE'S AN UNLIMITED NUMBER OF WAYS YOU CAN DECORATE A ROOM WITH PAPER. HERE ARE FOUR IDEAS TO GET YOU STARTED.

STRING OF STARS

Create delicate decorations by cutting out silhouette shapes such as stars, leaves or hearts, in finely patterned papers. Old maps and book pages work particularly well, but geometric and floral designs can look good too. Again, use cotton furnishing braids and glue, making sure you double up your paper silhouette with the pattern facing outwards and the braid sandwiched in between. Shorter decorative strings of paper silhouettes like these can be used to decorate window ledges, mirrors and walls, and add an elegant detail to any room.

COCKTAIL AND CUPCAKES TOPPERS

When you're having a party, presentation is everything. That's why paper decorations are the perfect way to add a spot of style to any celebration. Whether you want to make beautiful Bellini cocktails or customised cupcakes, these simple paper decorations provide the kind of dazzling details that will make your soiree stand out. All you need is a handful of cocktail sticks, glitter, a selection of papers cut into silhouetted shapes and some glue.

6 · 2 h · £ 10 ↓

PAPER BUNTING

Triangles, rectangles and circles of paper look fabulous when strung up in long lengths of 15m (50ft) or more. Paper bunting can be used to create textured canopies above dining areas and is a simple and cost effective way to add character to a room at large-scale events. You can use almost any type of paper – hand-dyed paper in a mix of hues works well, as does sheet music, old book pages and maps. We tend to use gold and neutral coloured cotton furnishing braids and a glue gun to make bunting, but you can also run paper through a sewing machine, so if you've got bunting tape to hand, try machine stitching. If you are using a sewing machine with paper, remember to use a fine cotton needle.

FIREPLACE SWAG

Once you're confident that you know how to make a paper wreath (see page 54), try making a fireplace swag. The only difference is the shape of the cardboard backing. Cut yours to size by measuring the length of your fireplace, and then fill in the leaves using the same process as for the wreath. Use malleable floristry wire to add pine cones or fresh berries and coloured paper ribbons to inject colour and warmth. Again, playing with scale can be a good way to create more unusual or quirky designs – a giant wreath could look fantastic in a window, while a series of tiny ones hung on ribbons would be perfect on a wall or mirror.

CAKE DECORATIONS

× **EVERYONE LOVES A BEAUTIFUL CAKE, BUT NOT EVERYONE HAS THE BAKING SKILLS TO WHIP UP PERFECT PUDDINGS AND CELEBRATORY SURPRISES AT THE DROP OF A HAT. SO, IF SUGAR CRAFT FEELS LIKE A STEP TOO FAR, HERE IS AN ALTERNATIVE WAY TO MAKE FABULOUS-LOOKING CAKES WITH SIMPLE PAPER DECORATIONS.**

GATHER YOUR INGREDIENTS
Hand-painted paper ribbons, delicate strings of tiny bunting, cocktail stick flags, and hand-crafted bows can all be used to decorate cakes. Use dressmaking pins to hold the decorations in place and a whole world of cake design opens up. Throw paper flowers into the mix and you have all the ingredients you need to make even the most basic sponge look spectacular.

ADD A DOLLOP OF COLOUR
Use bold colour combinations and striking patterns to make eye-catching creations. Traditional white icing sets off the coloured paper nicely and watercolour paints can be used to add an unusual level of texture to your design. Start by painting pattern samples on paper, and then hold up small swatches against the cake to get a sense of which combinations work best.

LET YOUR CAKE RISE TO THE OCCASION
Play with scale and use the decorations to add texture, volume and height to your cake. When arranging the decorations, think about creating harmonious compositions that have an overall sense of balance.

Et voilà! You've made a spectacular decorated cake without the need to enrol in a fancy pastry school.

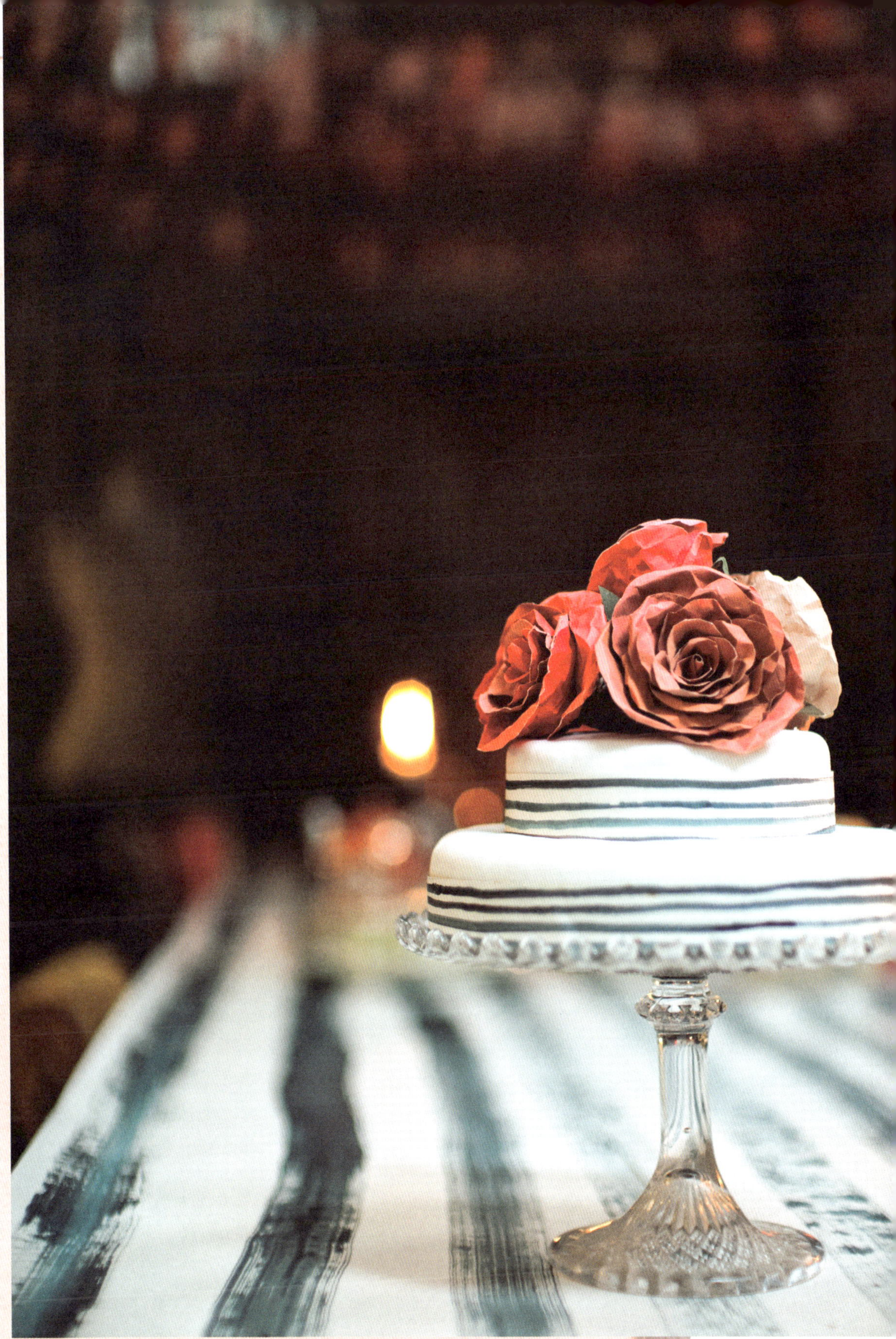

P·A·P·E·R W·R·E·A·T·H

× PAPER GARLANDS MAKE GREAT INTERIOR DECORATIONS NO MATTER WHAT THE SEASON. AT THE PARLOUR WE HANG THEM ON FIREPLACES, PIN THEM TO DOORS AND USE THEM TO ADORN MIRRORS. ONCE YOU FEEL CONFIDENT SCULPTING FLOWER HEADS, FEEL FREE TO GET EXPERIMENTAL WITH THE SIZE AND LAYOUT OF YOUR WREATHS. THINK CAREFULLY ABOUT COLOUR PALETTES BEFORE YOU BEGIN TO ENSURE TONES AND HUES ARE PERFECTLY MATCHED.

e

h 3

£ 10 ↓

WHAT YOU NEED

× Cardboard box
× Pencil
× Scissors
× 8 dried rose stems
× A selection of hand-dyed paper (see page 26)
× Glue gun and glue sticks
× Off-white lining paper
× Black paint

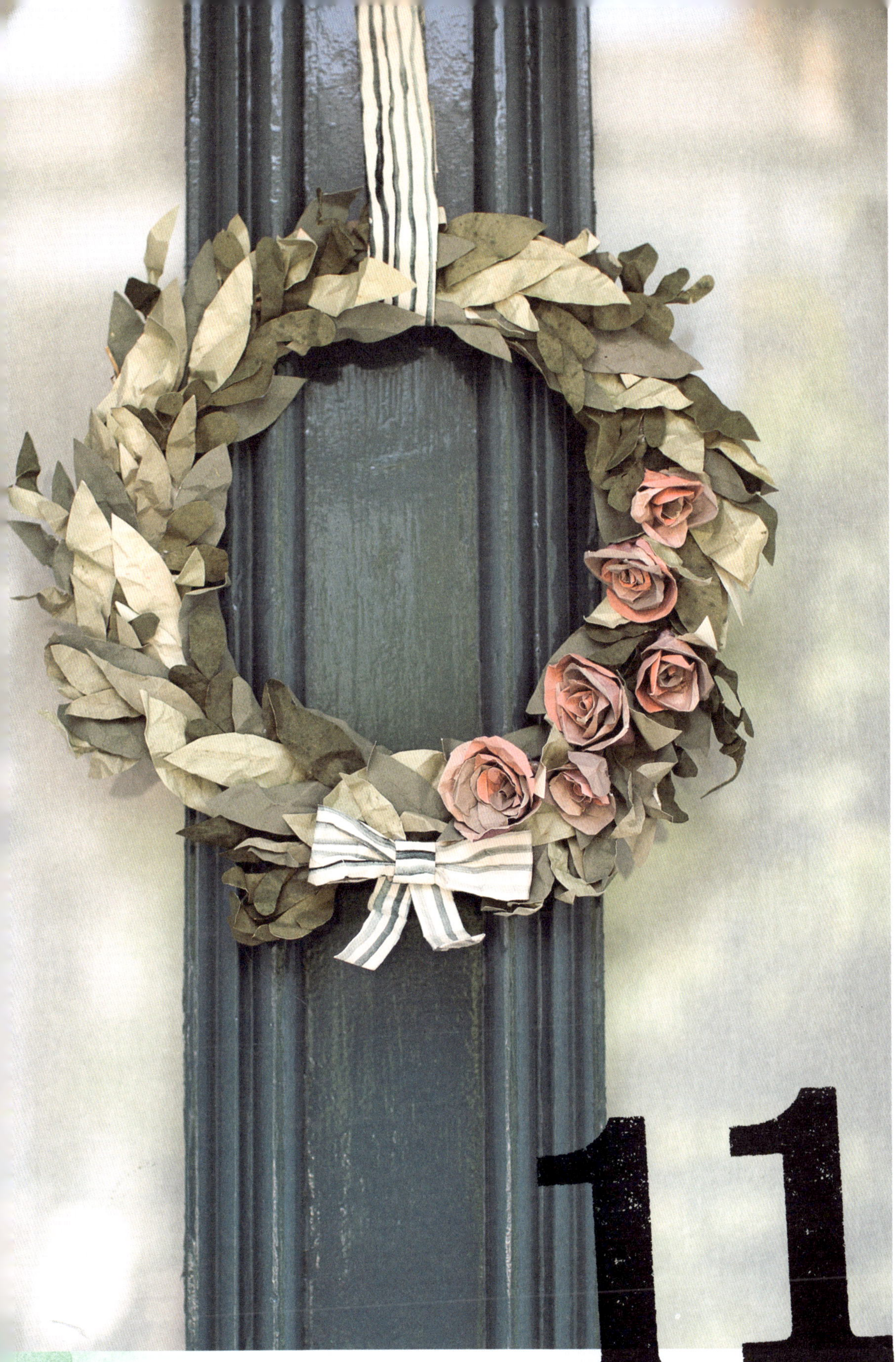

11

PAPER WREATH

1. Open out a cardboard box and place it on a flat surface. Lay a large plate or circular object on top of the cardboard sheet and draw a circle around the outside of the object. Using a ruler make a number of pencil marks around the outside of your circle measuring 5cm (2cm) from its edge. Join the pencil marks together using dash marks to form a second circle. Cut out the cardboard ring beginning with the outside edge, followed by the inside edge. This cardboard ring will form the basis of your garland.

2. Cut the dried rose stems into shorter lengths of approximately 20 x 7cm (8 x 2¾in) and 10 x 5cm (4 x 2in). Switch on your glue gun and start attaching the dried rose stems to the cardboard base following the pattern shown in image 02. Make sure you leave a slight gap at the top where your paper ribbon will go.

3. Once the flower stems are in place, create the hanging loop and attach the bow by following the paper ribbon steps, right.

4. With the ribbons in place it's time to begin adding the first layer of leaves. Cut out approximately 30 large dark green leaves measuring 4–5cm (1½–2in) in length, along with 50 smaller leaves 2–3cm (¾–1⅛in) in length and 40 rounded end leaves 3–4cm (1⅛–1½in) in length. Using the glue gun, begin attaching the leaves, roughly following the pattern shown.

5. Once every inch of the garland has been covered with leaves, make the roses (see page 30).

6. Attach the roses using the glue gun and add additional leaves where needed to ensure an even finish.

PAPER RIBBON

1. Take a piece of off-white lining paper measuring 30 x 20cm (12 x 8in) and paint a series of vertical black lines. Leave to dry, then cut into approximately three ribbons measuring 5cm (2in) wide x 30cm (12in) long. Create a 3mm (⅛in) fold over the long raw edges of each paper ribbon and secure with glue – this will give the ribbons a smooth edge.

2. Use the first strip of paper ribbon to make the garland's hanging loop. Fold the ribbon around the top of the garland and join the ends of the paper ribbon by folding the edges over one another like a parcel, then glue.

3. Next, use the second paper ribbon to make the main body of the bow. Fold the ribbon to form a continuous loop then flatten so that the join is in the middle. Glue in place then pinch the loop in at the centre to create a bow shape. Now secure with a smaller piece of paper ribbon around the middle.

4. Finally, use the third piece of paper ribbon to form the tail of the bow. Fold the ribbon to form a 45-degree angle then trim the edges by eye. Attach the back of the bow with a blob of glue.

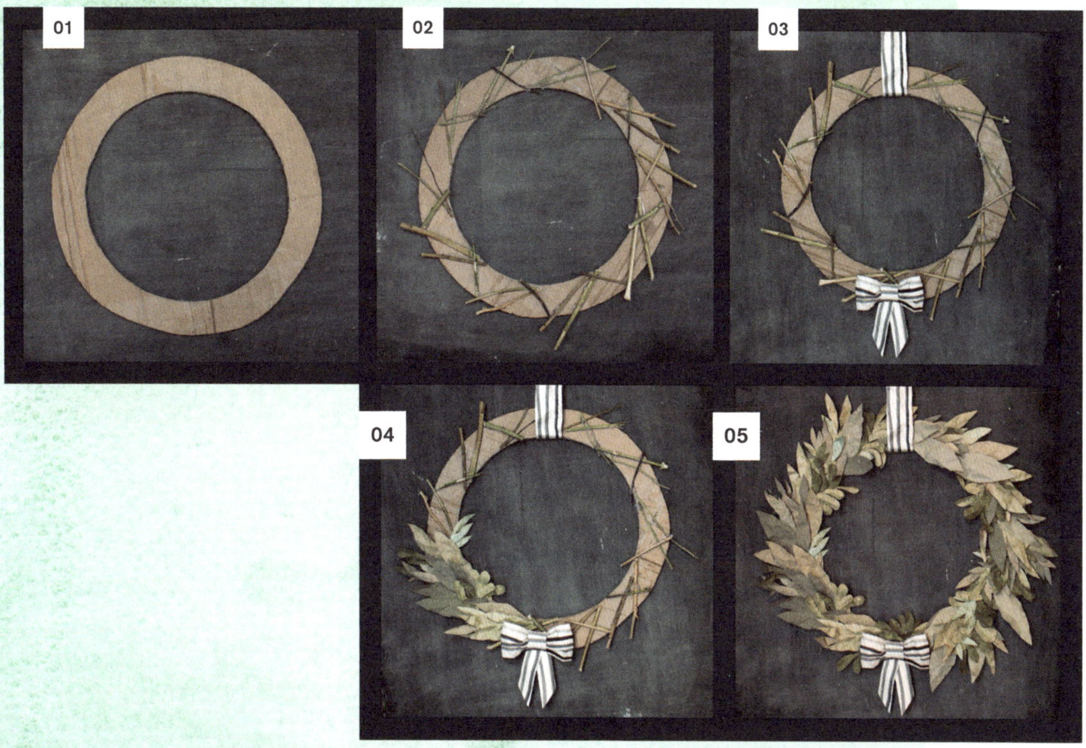
01
02
03
04
05

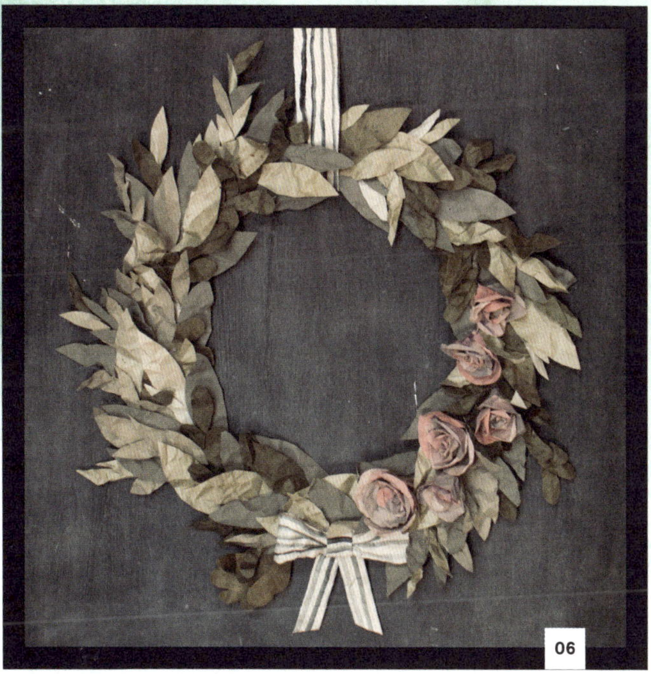
06

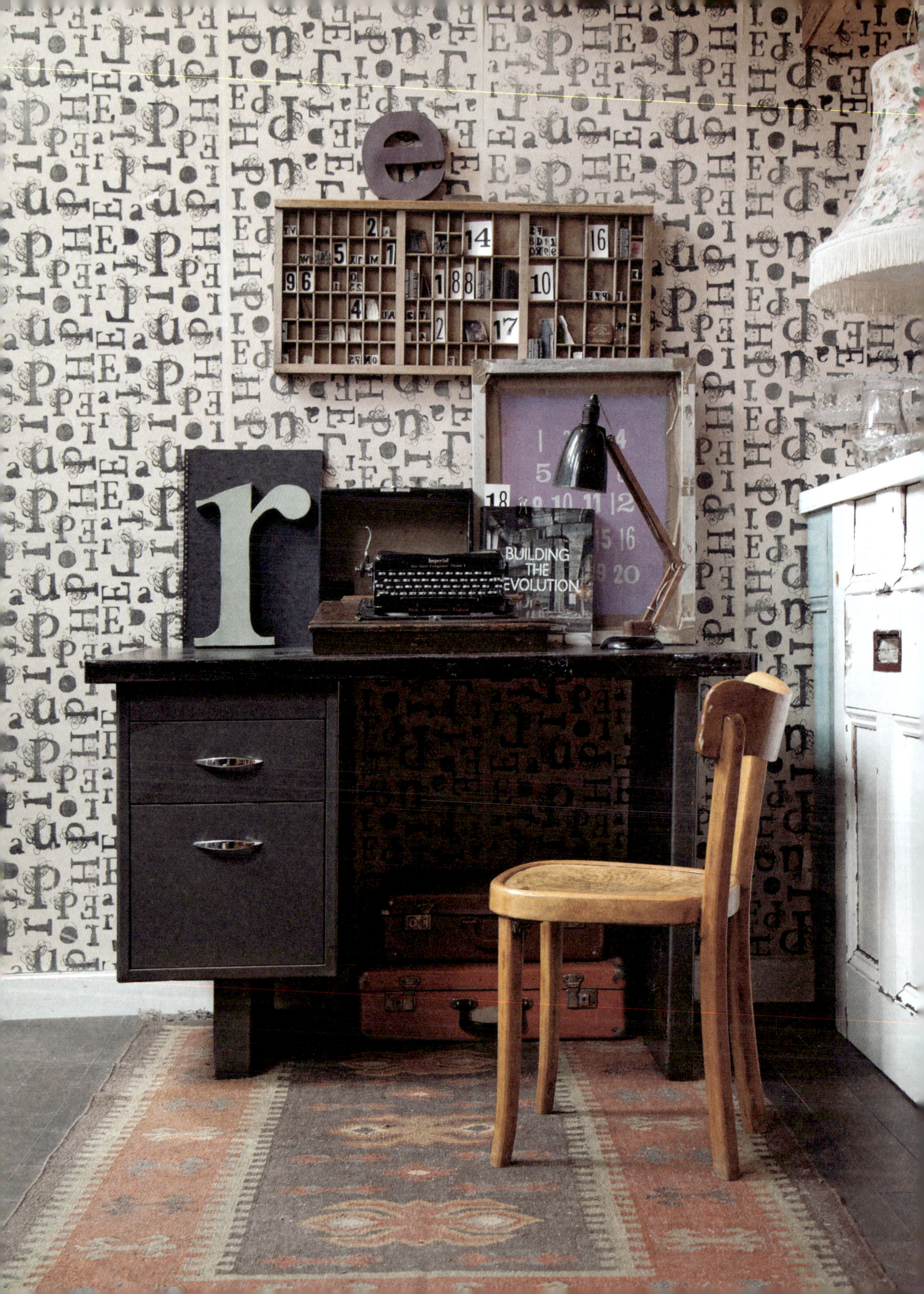
BUILDING THE EVOLUTION

12

3·D T·Y·P·O·G·R·A·P·H·Y

WHAT YOU NEED

- A letter or a number printed on an A4 sheet of paper
- 3 sheets of card (any will do)
- Some good-quality, high-pigment paint
- Pencil
- Ruler
- Scissors
- Glue gun and glue sticks

× LOOK THROUGH ANY INTERIOR DESIGN BOOK AND YOU WON'T HAVE TO SEARCH TOO LONG BEFORE YOU FIND LETTERS AND CHARACTERS FROM VINTAGE SHOP SIGNS BEING USED TO ADORN WALLS AND ADD STYLISH DETAILS TO ROOMS. WE LOVE FINDING EXAMPLES OF VINTAGE TYPOGRAPHY AT ANTIQUE MARKETS AND INTERIORS STORES, BUT WE DON'T LOVE THEIR PRICE TAG. HERE'S A SIMPLE WAY TO GET THE LOOK FOR MUCH, MUCH LESS.

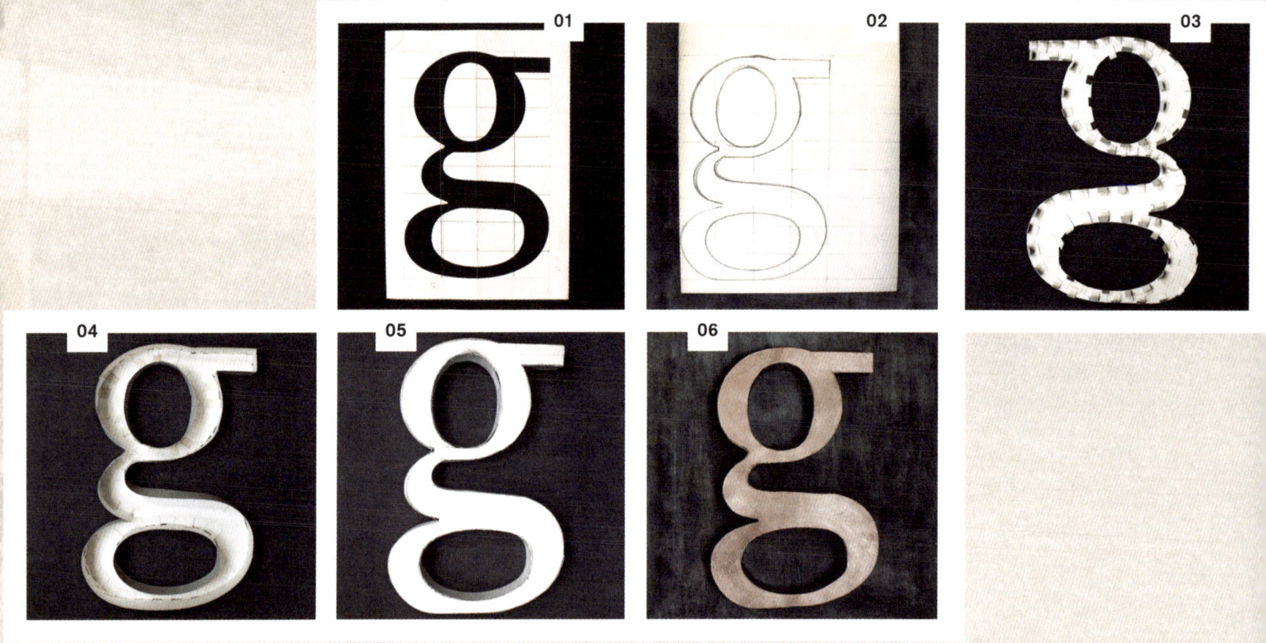
01
02
03
04
05
06

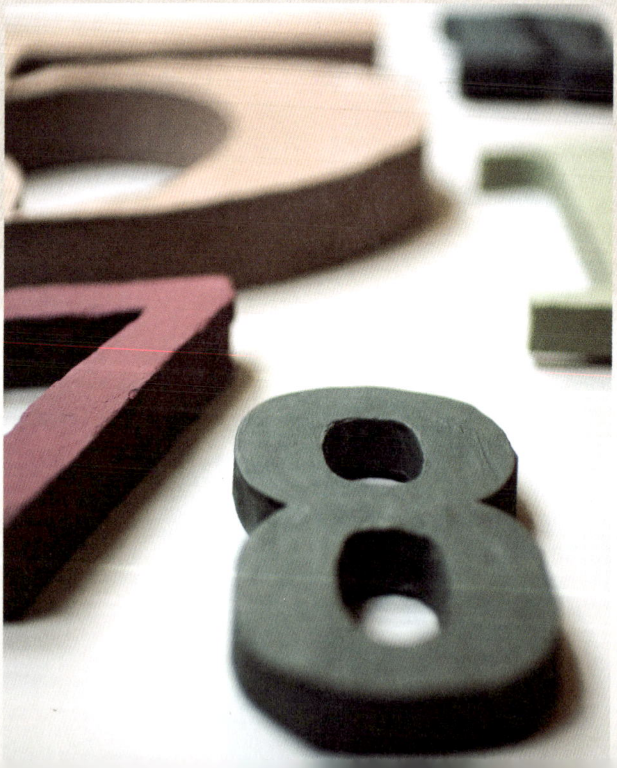

Don't spend money on expensive materials – use what you have to hand

1. Begin by finding a letter or number that you love the shape of. Try playing around with various fonts in a word processing program and find the ones that you think are most beautiful in terms of their shape and proportion. Blow your chosen character up to a good size and print it out on a piece of paper. Next draw a box around the outside of it. Measure the width of the character and split it into 4 even columns, then repeat the same process vertically to create a grid 8 rows deep.

2. Measure the length of each grid line, making a note of the overall width and height of the grid, along with the width and height of each of the grid's squares. Next, decide how big you want your 3D letter to be. For example, if you want it to be twice as big as your original letter multiply each measurement by two or, if you want it to be three times as big, multiply the measurement by three. Now take a sheet of card and draw a second grid using your enlarged measurements. You should end up with a grid that has the same proportions as the original grid only two or three times bigger. Returning to the original letter, cover up all but one of the grid squares using a couple of sheets of paper. Copy the shape that you see in the visible square in the corresponding square on your enlarged grid. Pay careful attention to where you draw your lines by checking your pencil marks intercept each grid line at the same place as the original. Repeat for each of the remaining squares until you have copied the entire letter. Finally, take a look at the overall shape and make any adjustments necessary so that your enlarged copy looks as close to the original shape as possible.

3. Once you have your completed letter, cut it out using a pair of scissors. This will be the front of the letter. Next draw around the cut-out letter on a second piece of card to create the back of the letter. Using offcuts of card, cut up a big pile of pieces measuring approximately 1 x 4cm (⅜–1½in). Fold each piece in half to form little tabs then stick in place.

4. Decide how wide you want your letter to be, then cut the remaining card into strips of your chosen width: 5cm (2in) may be suitable for smaller letters and 10cm (4in) for larger ones. Using your glue gun, start applying tabs all the way around the outside of your letter. Next attach the long strips of card to form the edges of the 3D letter gluing and moulding the curves and angles as you go.

5. Once the sides are on, repeat the process of adding tabs all the way around the edges of the letter. Then attach the front.

6. When the letter has been glued together, finish it off by painting the card with a good-quality, high-pigment paint. You could use acrylic-based paints left over from decorating.

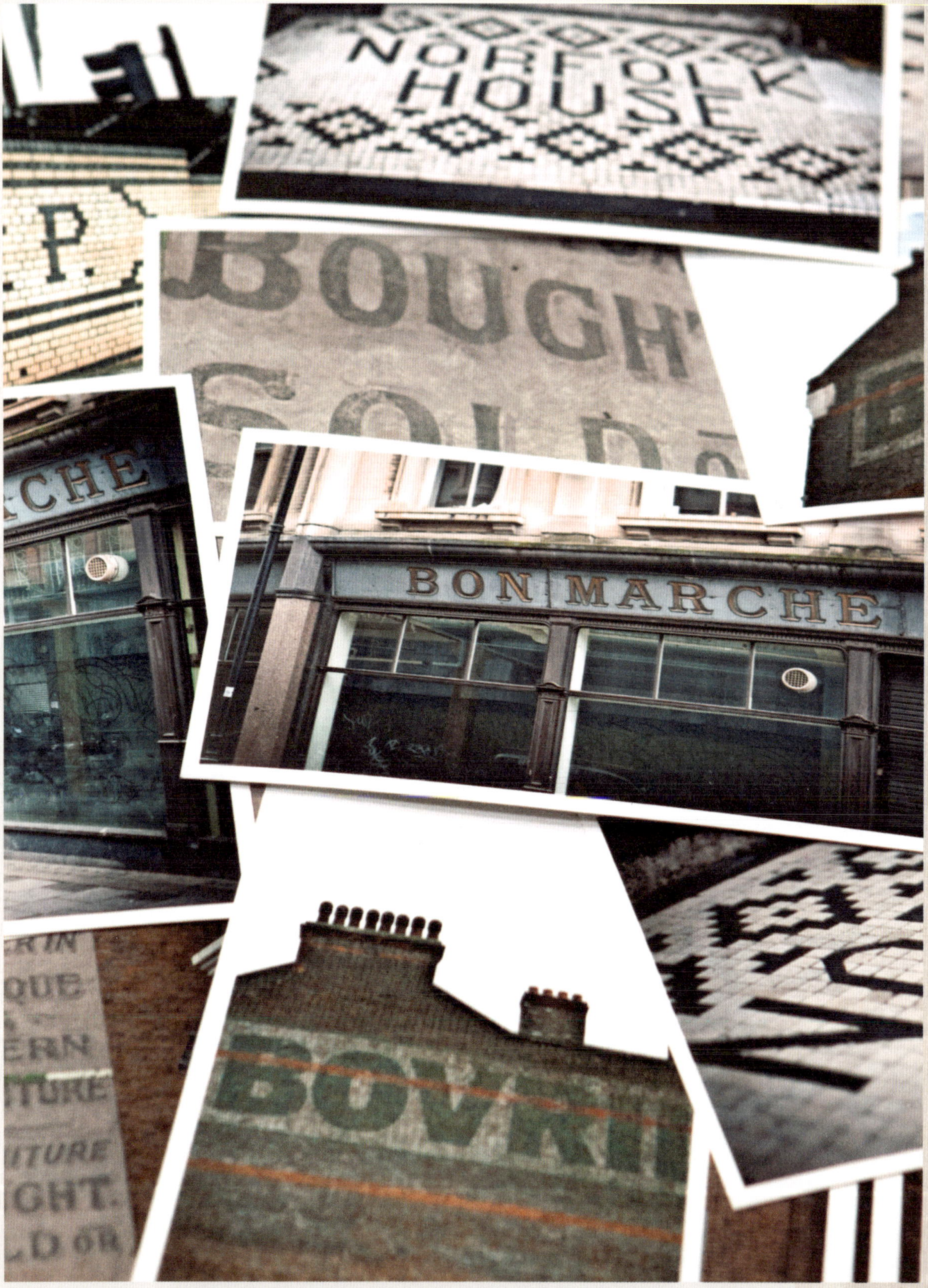
NORFOLK
HOUSE
BON MARCHE

TYPOGRAPHY WALK

× TYPOGRAPHY IS ALL AROUND US, BUT IT'S SOMETHING WE DON'T ALWAYS NOTICE. FIND INSPIRATION FOR YOUR 3D TYPOGRAPHY BY FOLLOWING THE INSTRUCTIONS BELOW – WE GUARANTEE YOU'LL FIND A WORLD OF EXTRAORDINARY FONTS RIGHT ON YOUR DOOR STEP.

1. Start where you are right now. In no more than 3 minutes, find five examples of interesting typography that you are attracted to. Notice the specific design details in each of the letters and fonts and make a mental note of which shapes you like best. Imagine you're putting on a special pair of graphic design glasses that make typography stand out from everything else.

2. Grab your coat and a camera and head off down the street. Don't plan a route for your walk – let the typography lead the way. From packaging and advertising to shop signs and architectural brickwork, follow the typographic trail from one example to the next, taking photos when you find elements you like.

3. When you've seen enough, go home and print out your photos. Arrange them in a sketchbook and think about how you could use your photographic fragments as a starting point for a design.

WHAT YOU NEED

× Coat
× Shoes
× Camera

m 30

£ 1 ↓

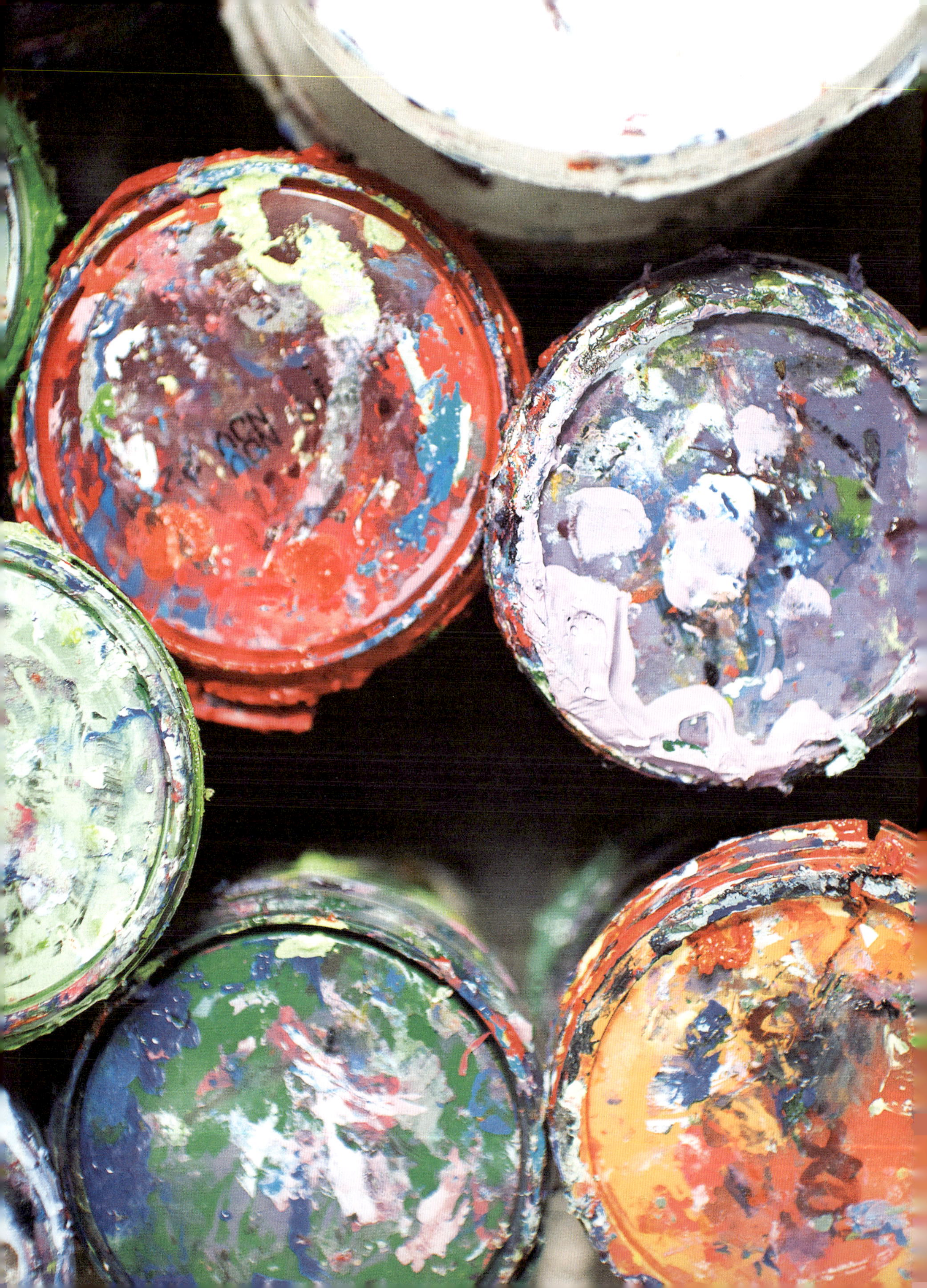

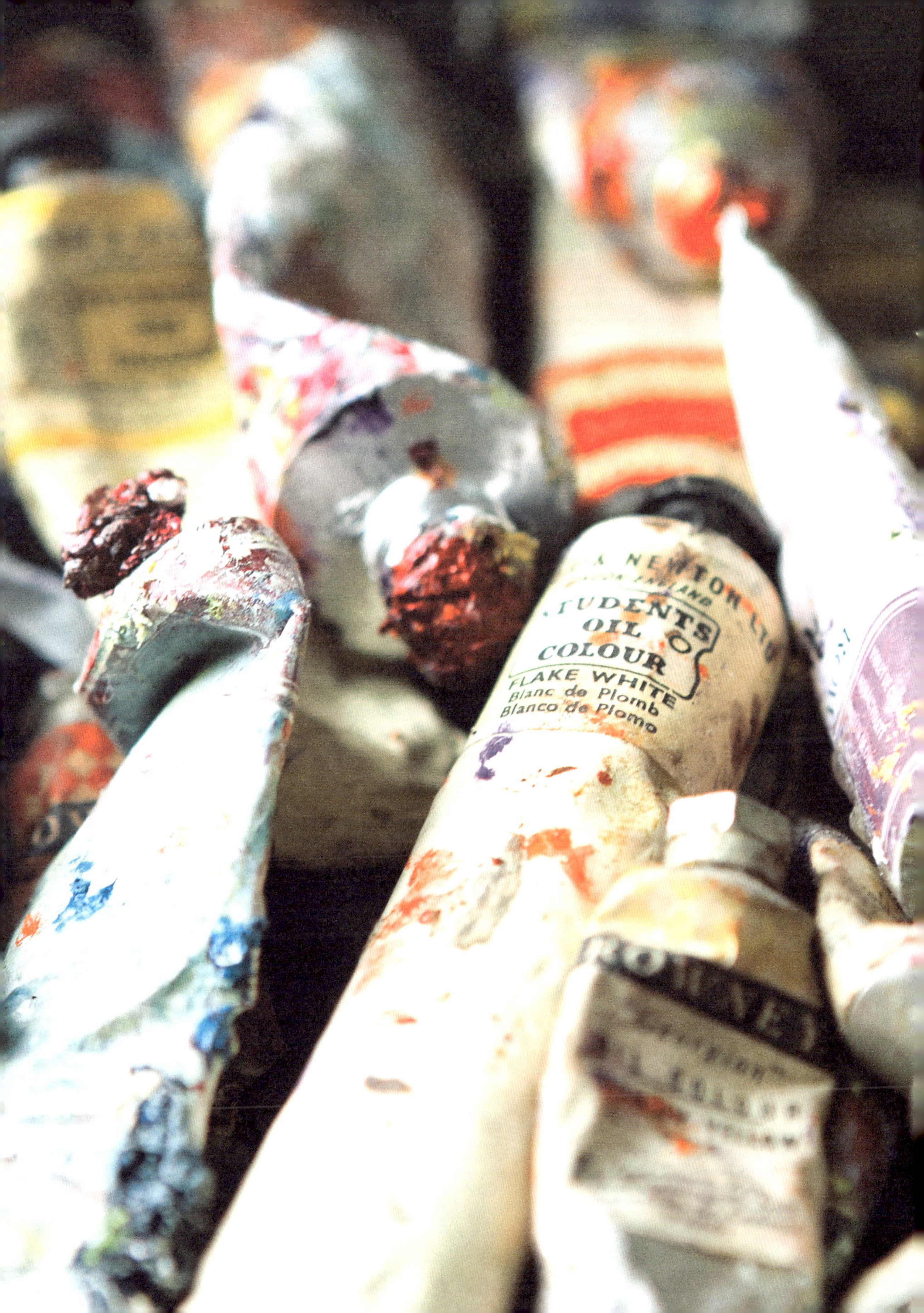
STUDENTS
OIL
COLOUR
FLAKE WHITE
Blanc de Plomb
Blanco de Plomo

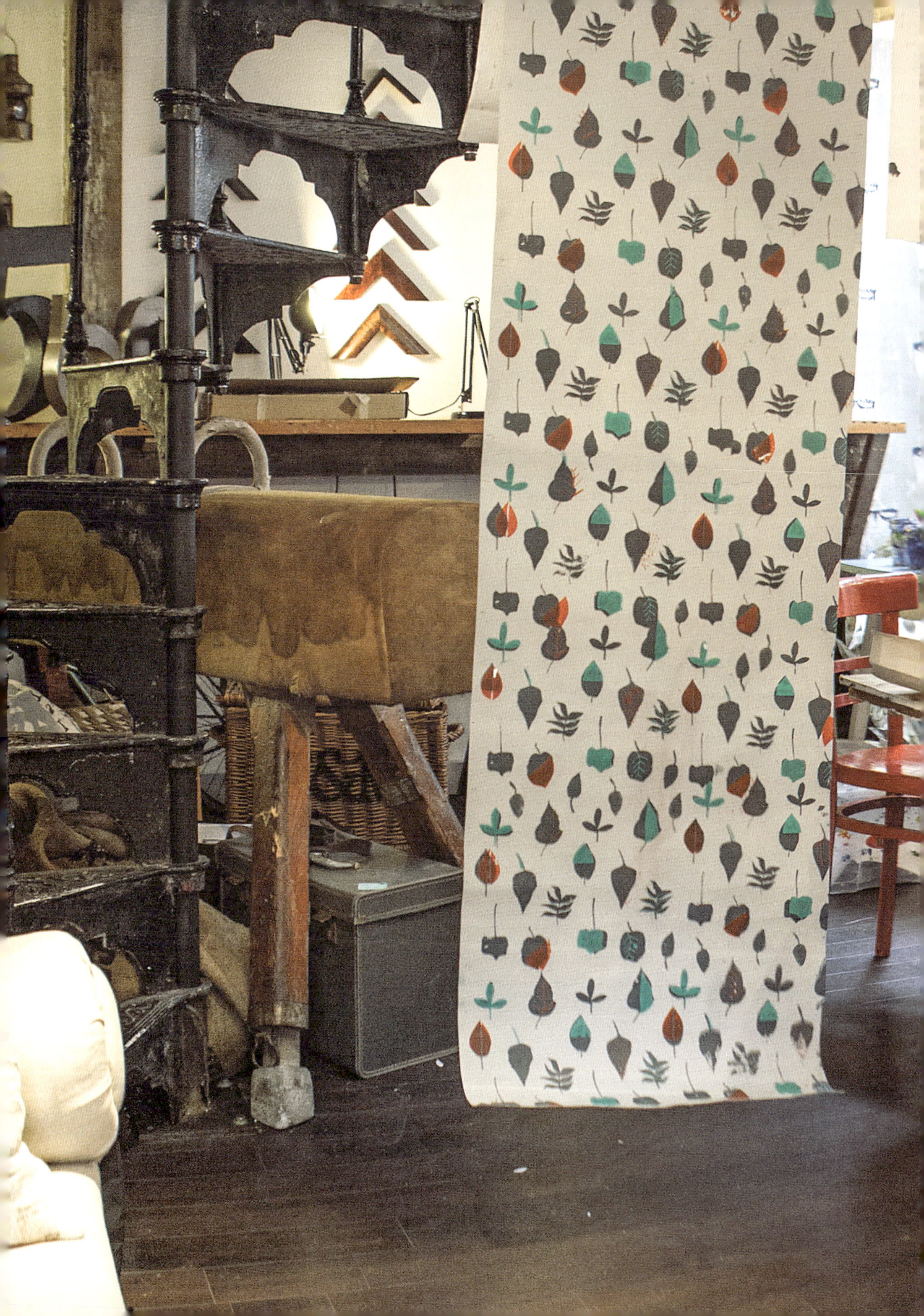

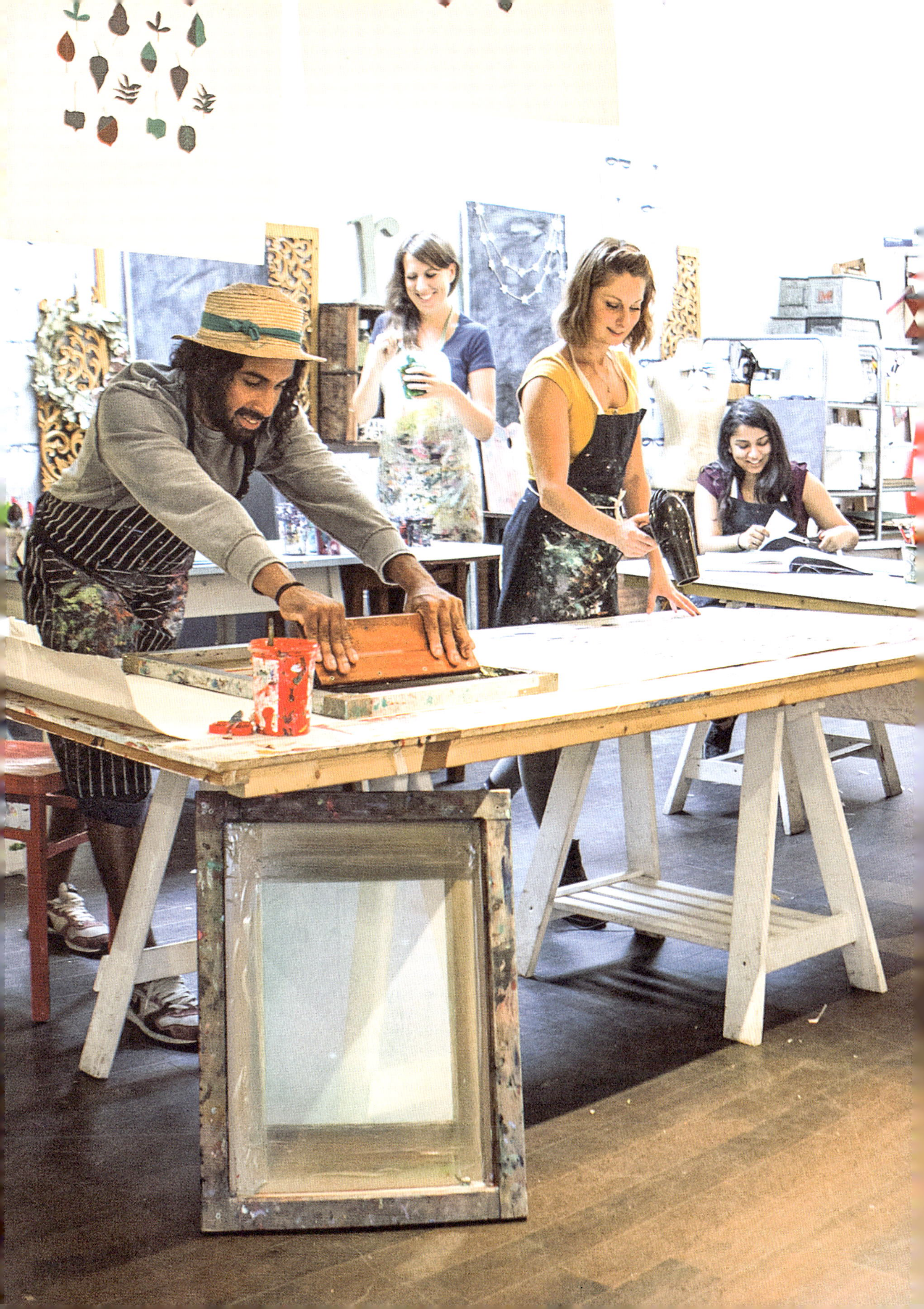

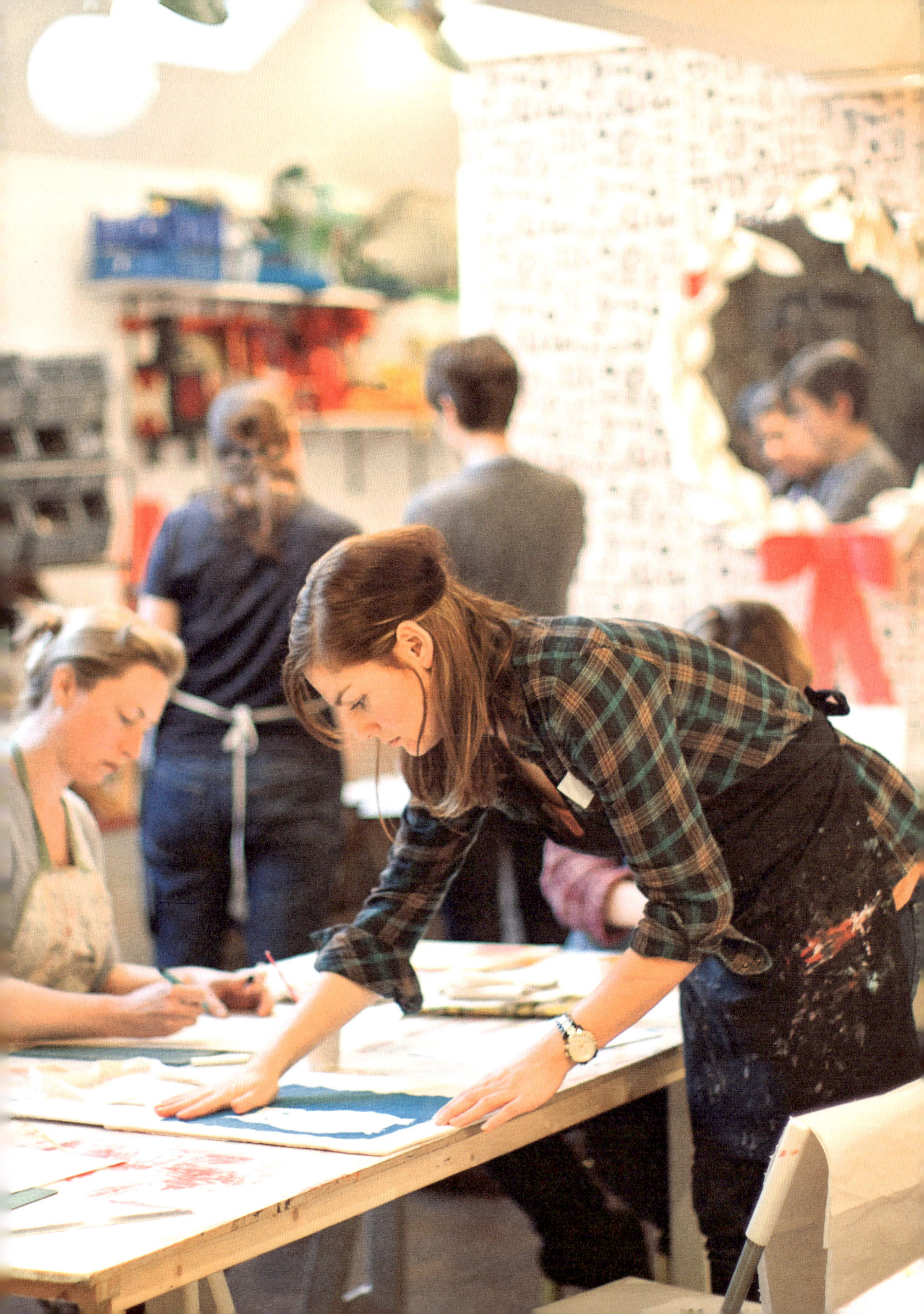

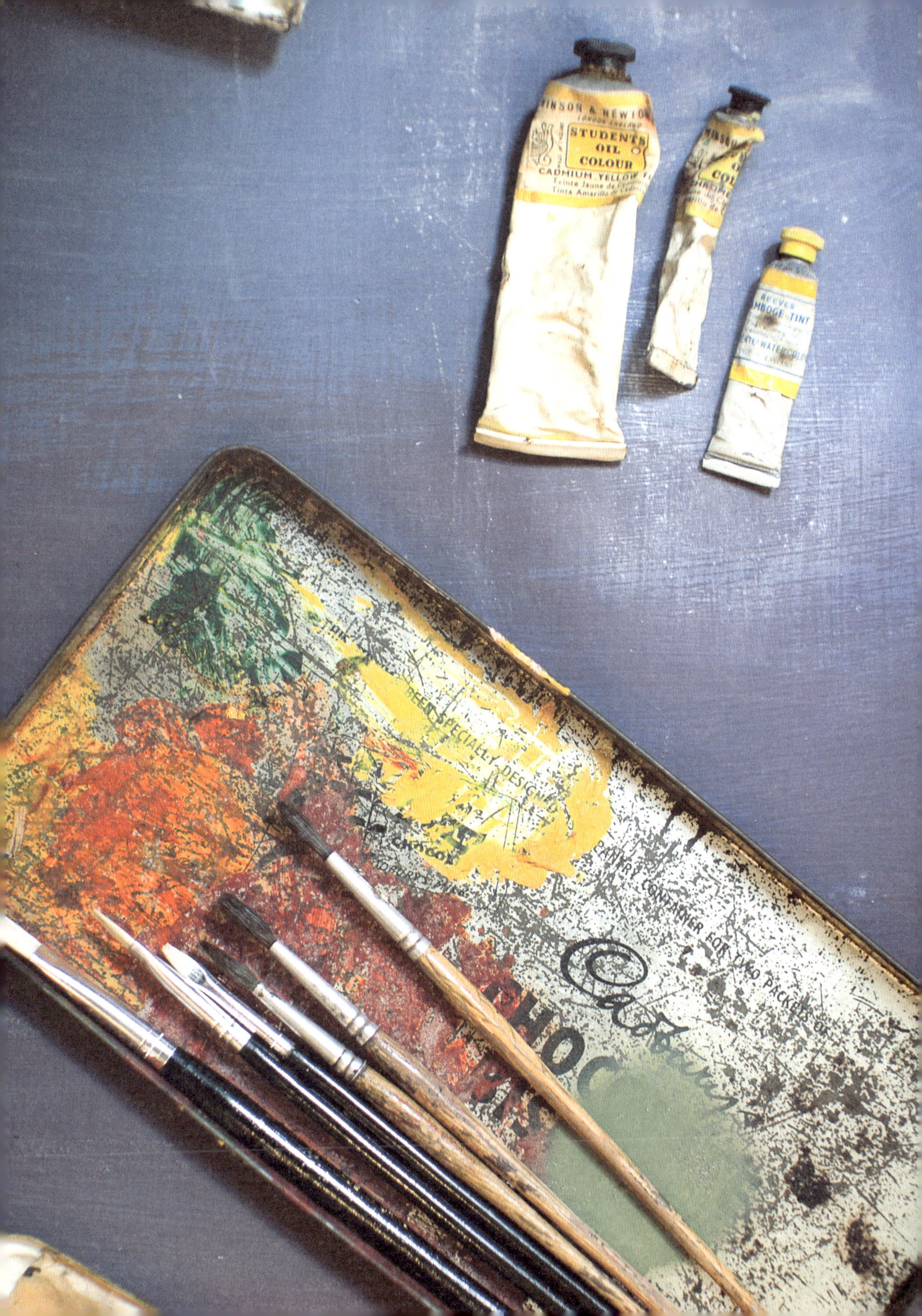
STUDENTS
OIL
COLOUR
BEEN SPECIALLY DESIGNED
CONTAINER FOR TWO PACKETS OF

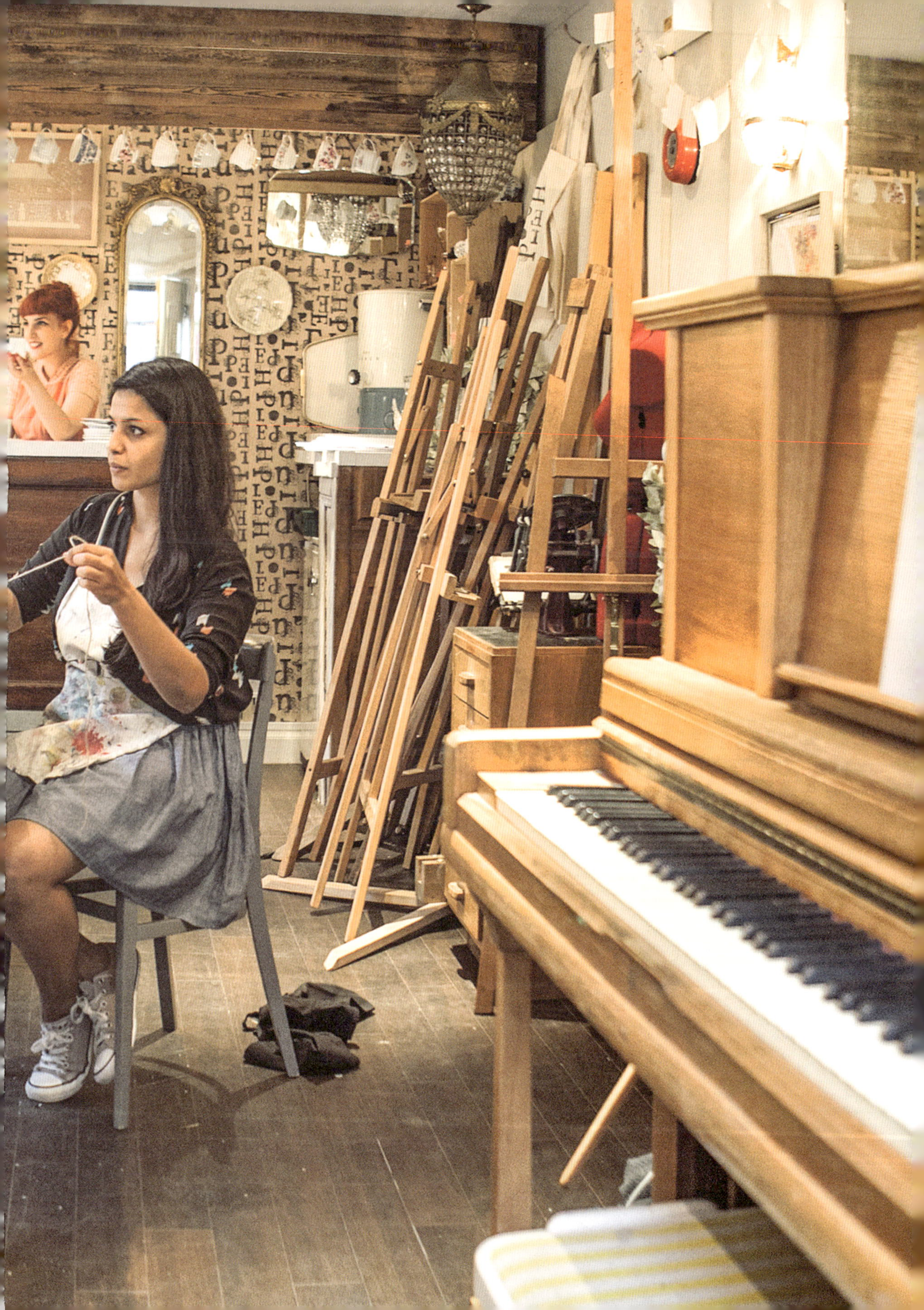

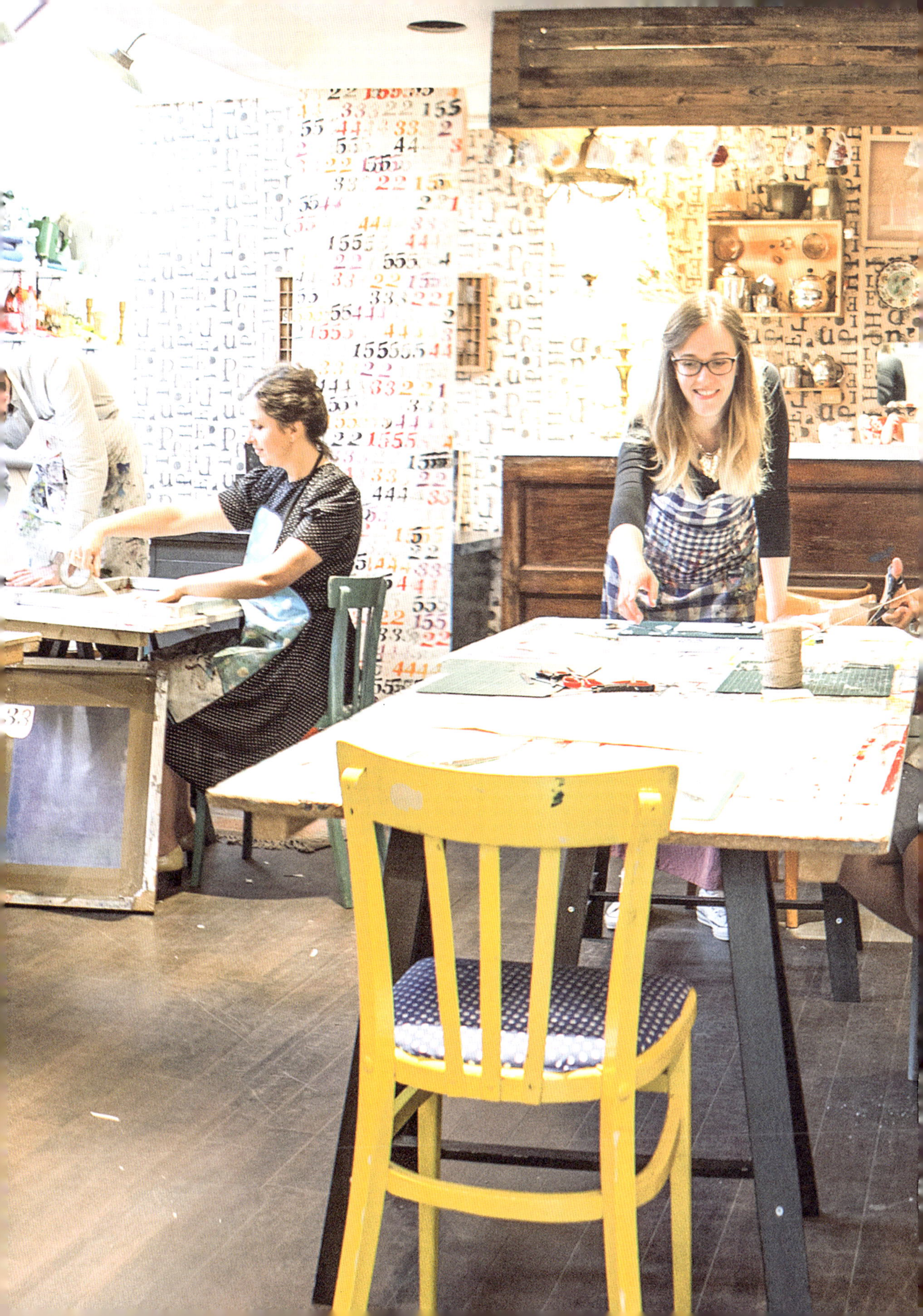

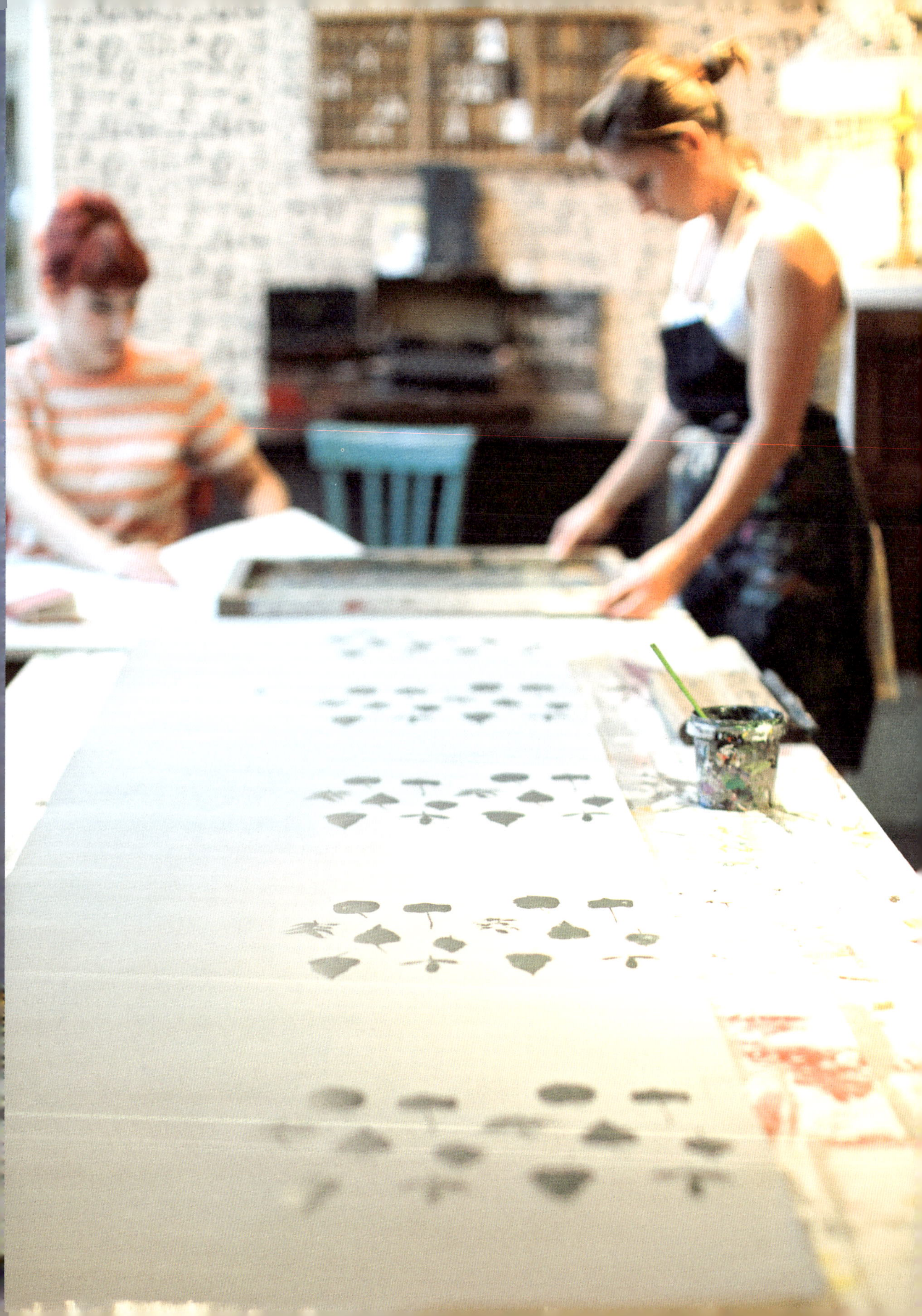

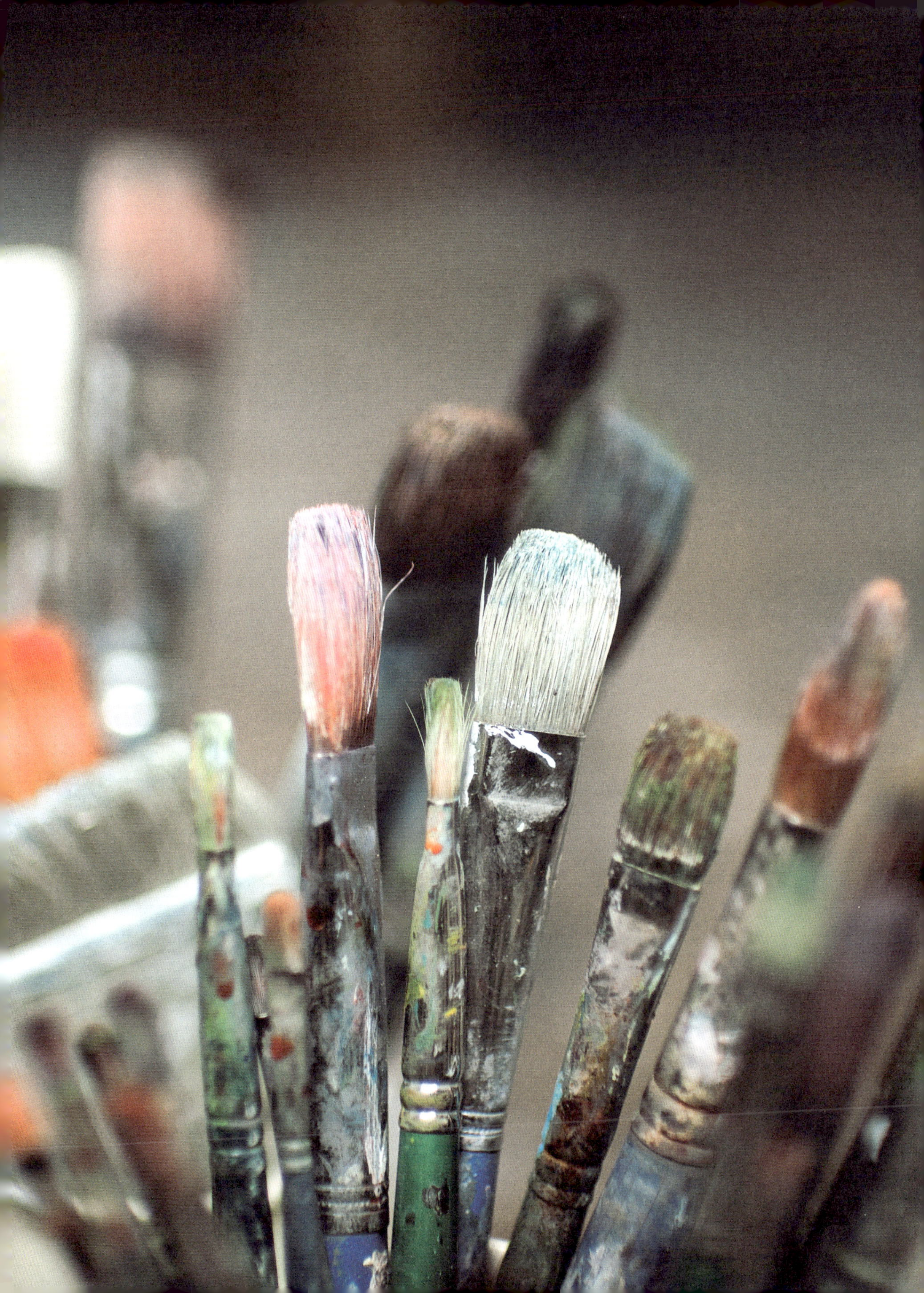

Try new things, test
ideas, take risks,
try new things, test
ideas, take risks

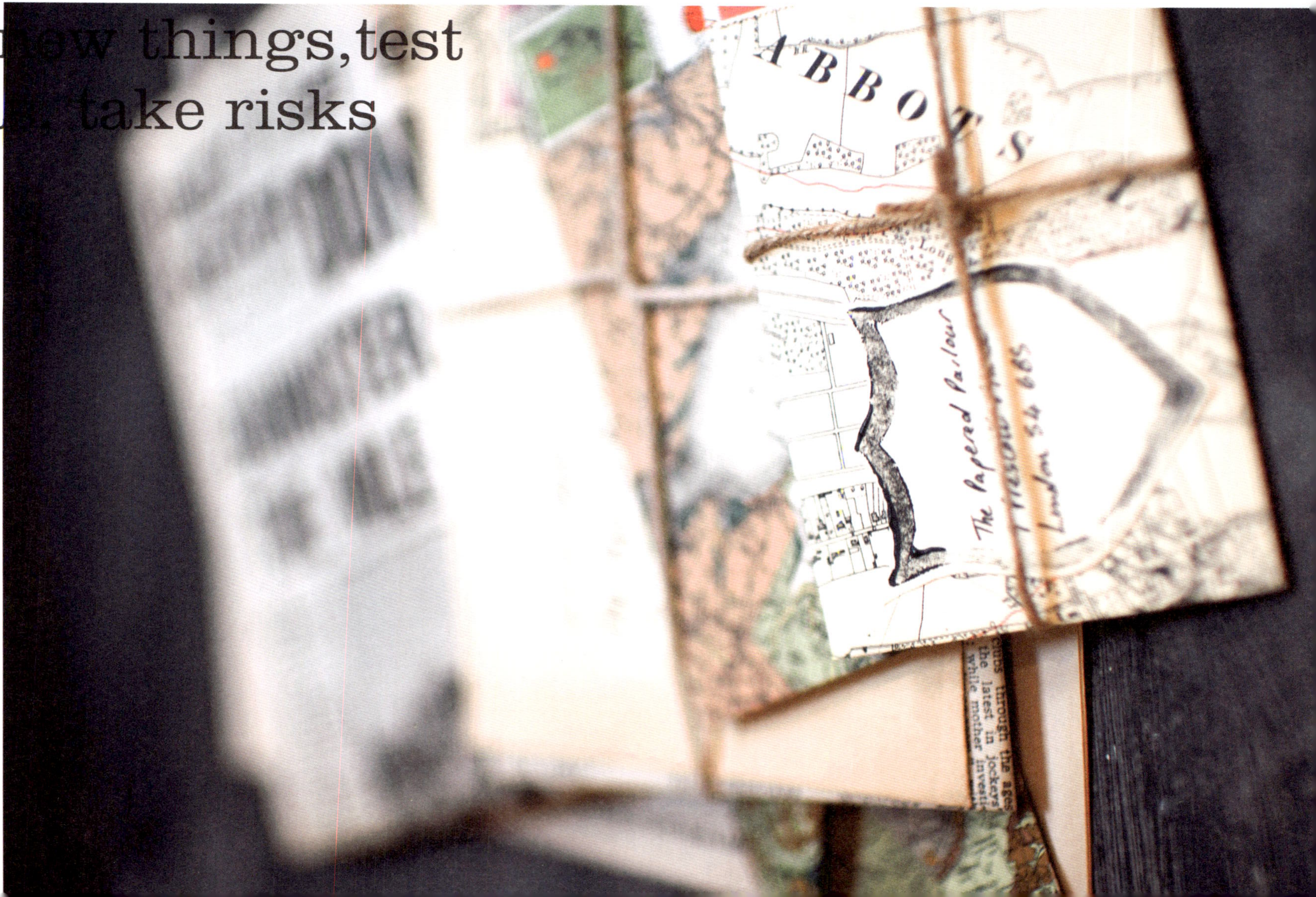

13

C·L·A·R·I·F·Y Y·O·U·R C·R·E·A·T·I·V·E G·O·A·L·S

× KICK START YOUR CREATIVITY BY TAKING A LITTLE TIME TO CLARIFY YOUR CREATIVE GOALS. THIS MAY SEEM SIMPLE, BUT IF YOU DON'T GET ALL THE PIECES OF THE PUZZLE IN PLACE FROM THE START YOU CAN END UP WITH AN INCOMPLETE PICTURE LATER ON. AVOID DESIGN DISASTERS BY RUNNING THROUGH THIS SIMPLE EXERCISE.

1. Take five minutes to think about your creative aspirations. Just spend a few moments musing over the ways you might like to add a little creativity to your daily life.

2. Now spend about five minutes getting your creative aspirations down on the page. It might come out as a short, bullet-pointed list, as a long stream of consciousness – a scribbled picture or just one key word. There is no right or wrong way to do it – do whatever feels good.

3. Review what you've written or drawn and make sure that somewhere you've made a positive statement about what you want. Try underlining a key phrase or adding a title to make the part about what you want really clear.

4. Finally, check that you've included a few specific details about how you'll know when you've reached your goal creatively, and what kind of resources you're going to need along the way to get you where you want to be.

5. When you're sure you've got it all down on paper, put your note in an envelope and send it to yourself in the post. When it arrives back on your doorstep, put the envelope somewhere safe to serve as a little daily reminder to take another step towards your creative dream.

6. If you're feeling confident about your ideas and don't mind sharing them with others, why not find a friend who you can begin a correspondence with. Having someone who can encourage you can sometimes be just the kind of support you need to get your creative aspirations off the ground.

WHAT YOU NEED

- A piece of paper
- Pen
- Envelope
- Postage stamp

6 | m 15 | £ 5 ↓

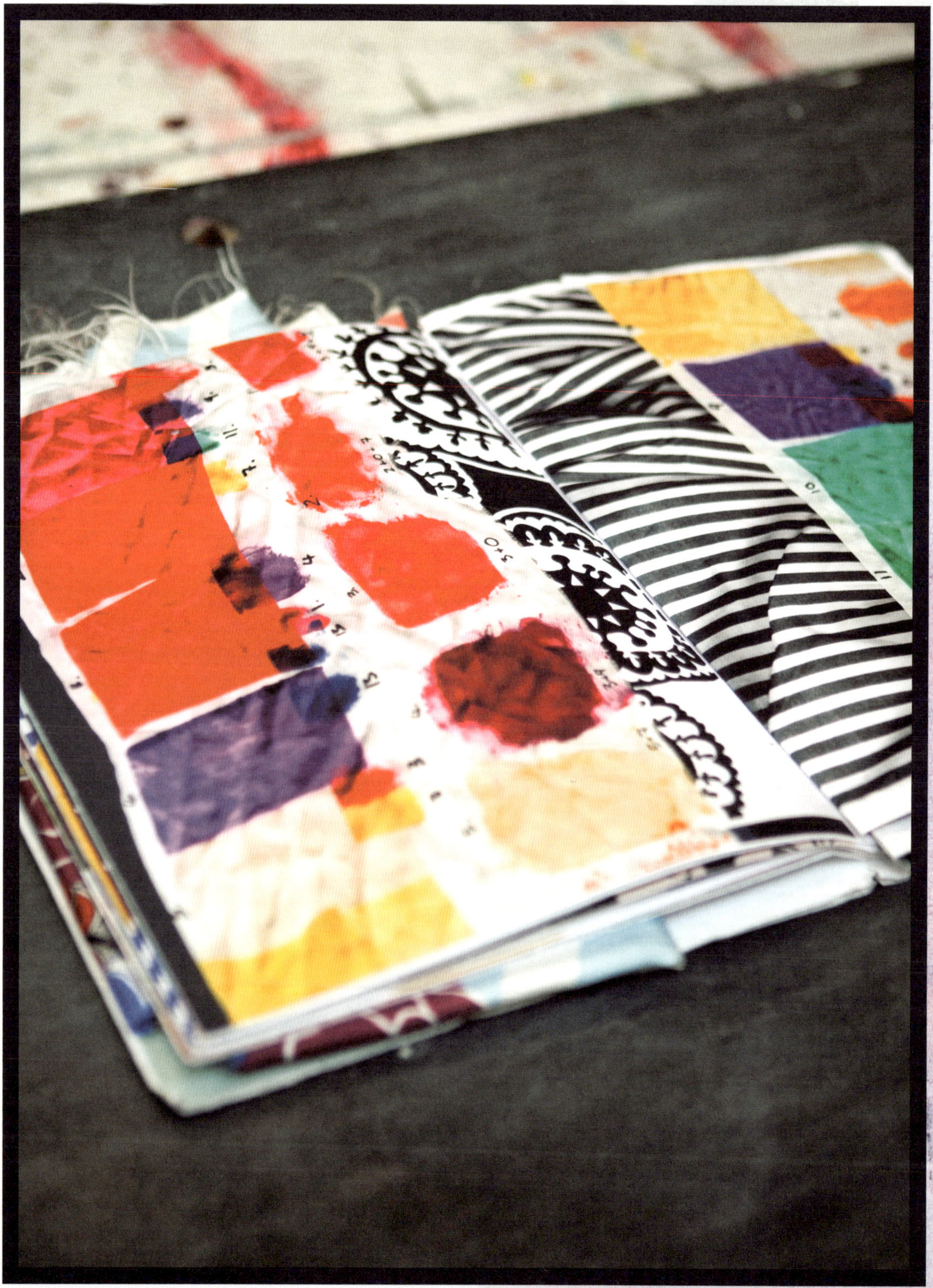

WHAT YOU NEED

- Sketchbook
- Pencils
- Pen
- Scissors
- Glue
- Box of paints

14

S·T·A·R·T Y·O·U·R O·W·N S·K·E·T·C·H·B·O·O·K

× A SKETCHBOOK IS A GREAT PLACE TO GATHER TOGETHER IDEAS AND BEGIN DEVELOPING YOUR OWN DESIGNS. ARTISTS USE SKETCHBOOKS AT EACH STAGE OF THE DESIGN PROCESS TO RECORD AND DEVELOP CONCEPTS BY DRAWING AND WRITING ABOUT THE THINGS THAT INSPIRE THEM. SOME ARTISTS TAKE A RELAXED APPROACH TO SKETCHBOOKS, STICKING THINGS IN AT RANDOM, WHILE OTHERS TREAT SKETCHBOOKS AS WORKS OF ART IN THEMSELVES. KICK-START YOUR CREATIVITY BY MAKING A SKETCHBOOK. HERE ARE FIVE STEPS TO HELP GET YOU GOING.

1. RECORD
A sketchbook can be a place for recording ideas that you find in the world around you. When anthropologists study different cultures they keep detailed field notes of their observations. Imagine you are an ethnographer and use your sketchbook as a place to record and observe the things you find interesting or inspiring.

2. SKETCH
Keep a small pocket book and pen with you at all times so you can practice your sketching skills on the fly. Don't worry if you're not that good at first – drawing skills develop over time; it's just a matter of practice.

3. COLLECT
Sketchbooks can be a great place for collecting and arranging bits and pieces found on your travels. Try using your sketchbook as a place for cataloguing and displaying your finds. Begin by grouping similar items according to colour, size or shape. Then use your collections as inspiration for colour pallets, patterns or compositions.

4. DEVELOP
Once you've finished experimenting with different designs, sketchbooks can become a great place in which to distil, display and collate your strongest ideas. Imagine the white pages of your sketchbook are gallery walls – only retain and display the designs you are most proud of.

5. NARRATE
Use your sketchbook to tell a story. Begin with the seed of an idea and then help it to grow through sketching, writing and marking the pages. Allow your ideas to develop from beginning to end until you have some kind of a narrative. When your designs can tell a story, you'll know they are fully formed.

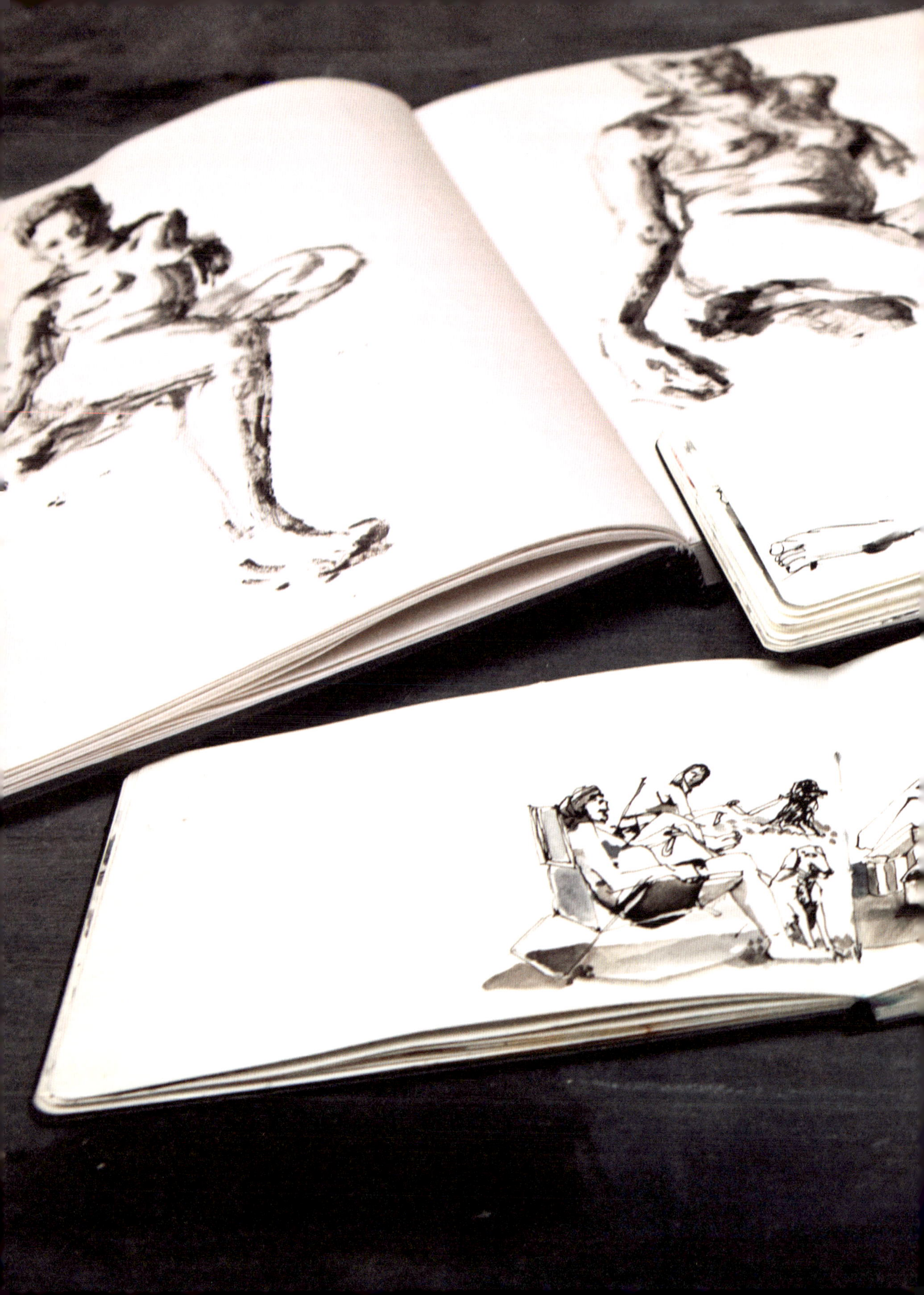

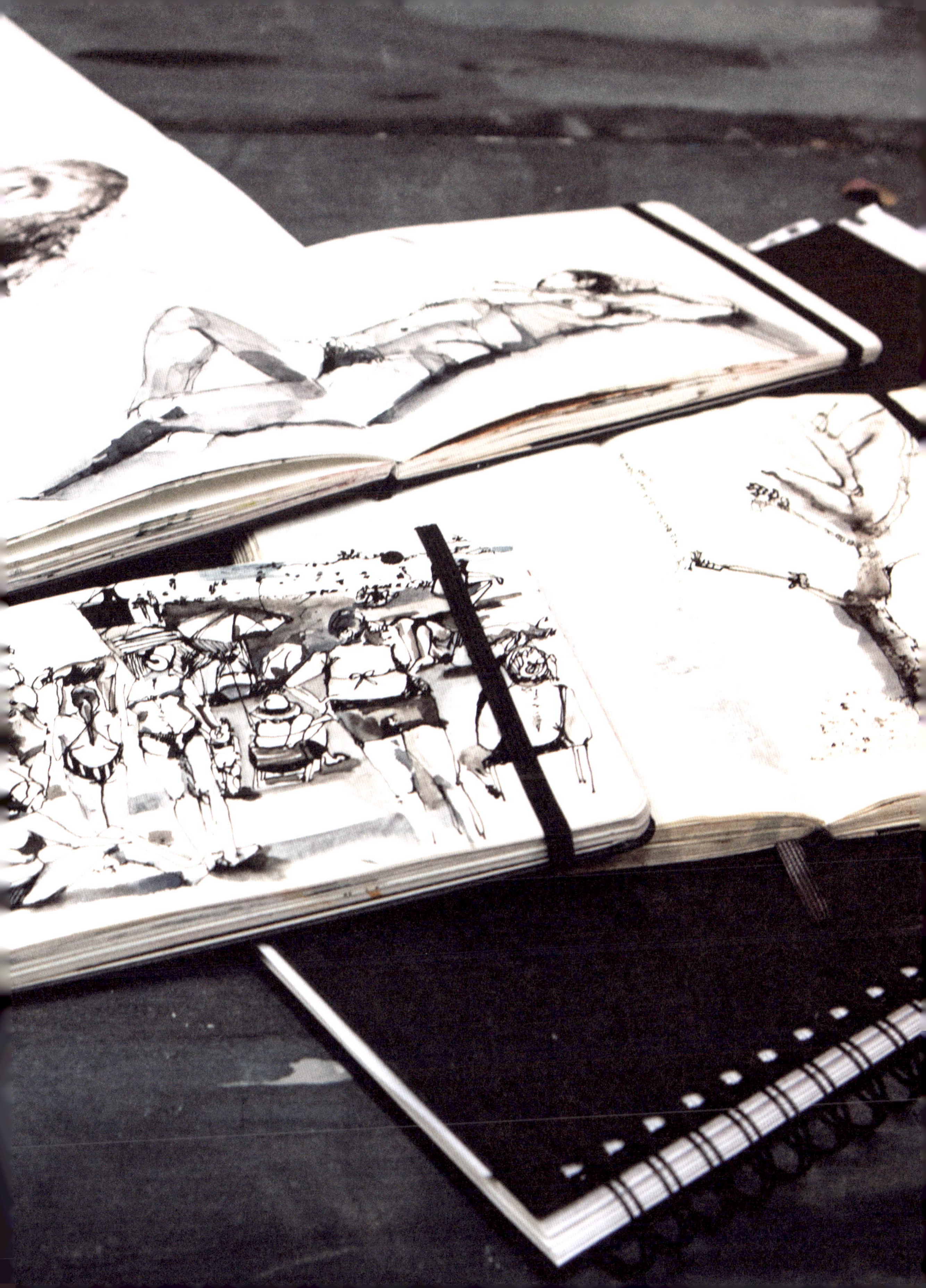

DEVELOPING YOUR OWN DESIGNS

× ALL WORKS OF VISUAL ART ARE MADE UP OF A NUMBER OF DIFFERENT DESIGN ELEMENTS. WHEN DEVELOPING DESIGNS IN YOUR SKETCHBOOK, TRY EXPERIMENTING WITH ELEMENTS FROM THE LIST BELOW. PICK ONE OR TWO ELEMENTS AT A TIME AND USE THEM AS A STARTING POINT TO TWEAK OR DISTORT SPECIFIC QUALITIES IN YOUR ROUGH SKETCHES. CONTINUE TO ADJUST YOUR INITIAL DESIGNS UNTIL YOU BEGIN TO GET INTERESTING RESULTS YOU FEEL PROUD OF.

- Colour
- Pattern
- Texture
- Line
- Shape (2D)
- Rhythm
- Proportion
- Composition
- Balance
- Variety
- Emphasis
- Contrast
- Scale
- Hierarchy
- Perspective

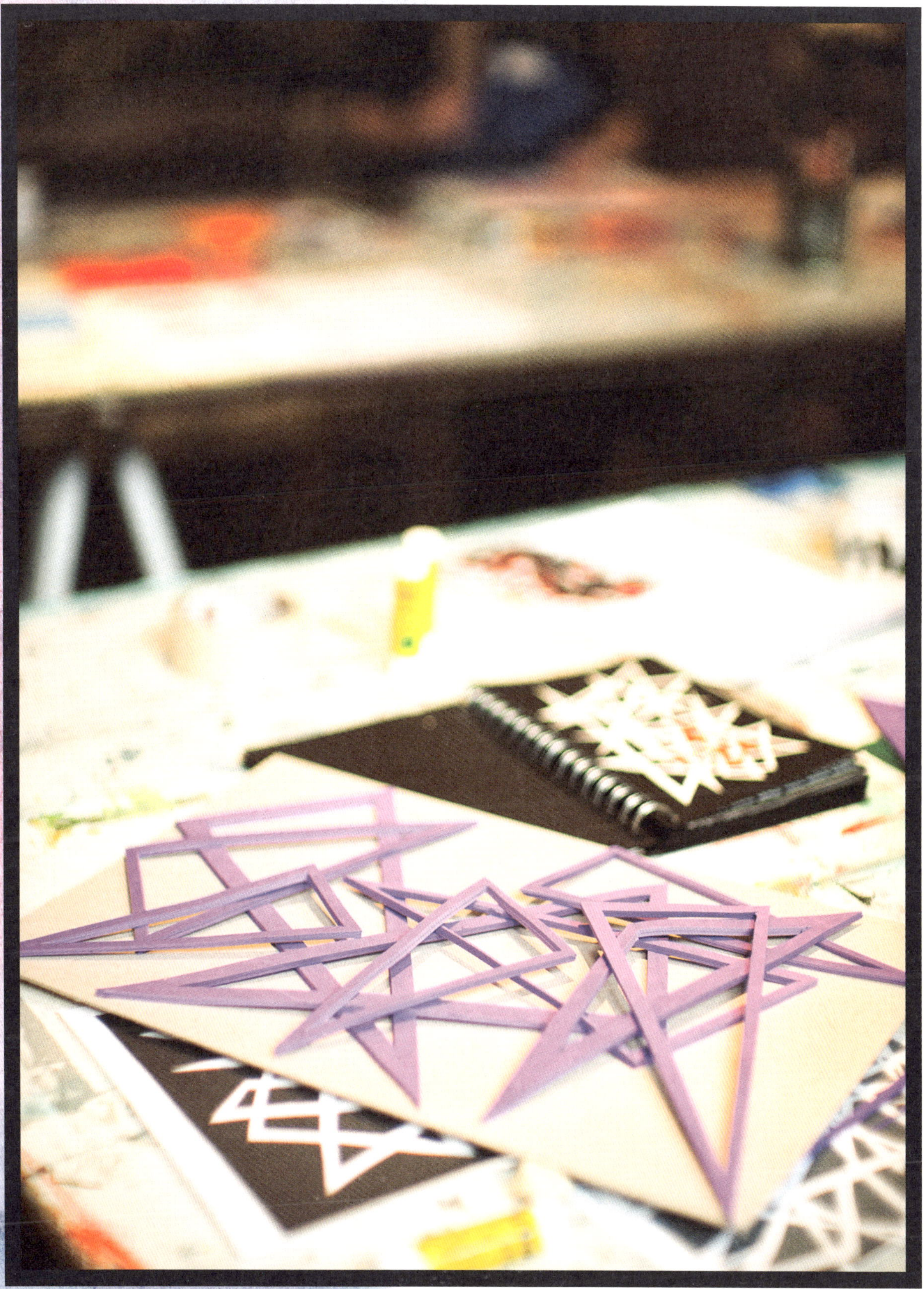

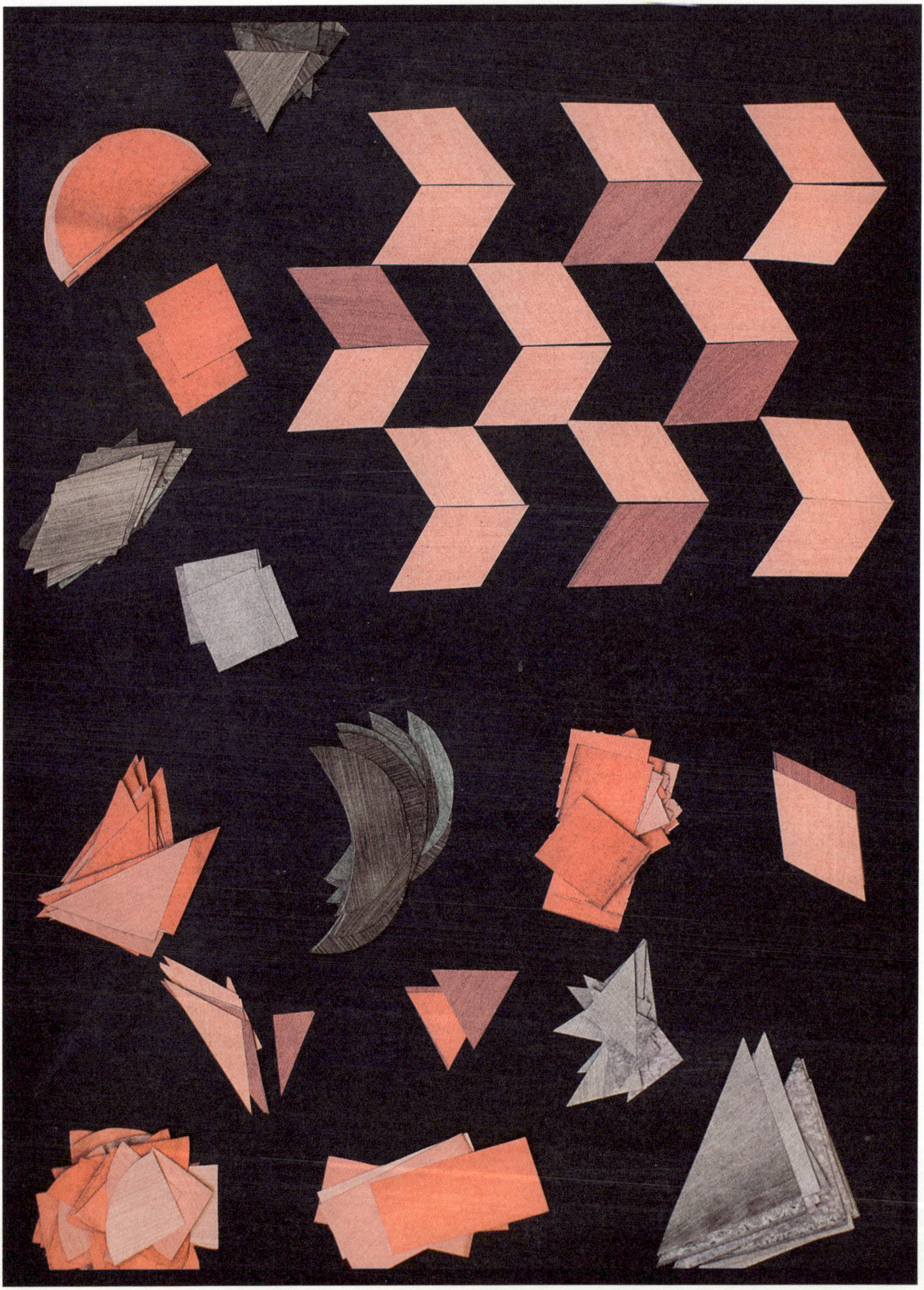

15

D·E·S·I·G·N A G·E·O·M·E·T·R·I·C P·A·T·T·E·R·N

WHAT YOU NEED

- Coloured card or paper
- Pencil
- Ruler
- Eraser
- Scissors

h 1-3

£ 5 ↓

× THIS GEOMETRIC PATTERN GENERATOR IS A SIMPLE WAY TO EXPLORE THE BASICS OF PATTERN DESIGN. ALL PATTERNS, NO MATTER HOW COMPLEX THEY SEEM AT FIRST GLANCE, HAVE AN UNDERLYING STRUCTURE THAT FALLS INTO THREE KEY CATEGORIES: REGULAR REPEAT, HALF-DROP REPEAT OR MULTIPLE-DROP REPEAT. THIS EXERCISE WILL HELP YOU TO IDENTIFY DIFFERENT TYPES OF PATTERN STRUCTURE SO YOU CAN START DESIGNING YOUR OWN GEOMETRIC PATTERNS, WHICH YOU CAN LATER TURN INTO WRAPPING PAPER OR WALLPAPER. THE MAIN AIM OF THIS PROJECT IS TO HAVE FUN PLAYING AROUND. SO MAKE YOURSELF A CUP OF TEA AND GIVE YOURSELF A BIT OF TIME JUST TO EXPLORE AND FIND OUT WHAT YOU CAN DO WITH A FEW BITS OF COLOURED CARD. WHEN YOU'VE HAD ENOUGH, PUT YOUR WORK ASIDE FOR A FEW DAYS AND REVISIT IT WHENEVER YOU FEEL LIKE IT.

1. Take a sheet of card and using a pencil and a ruler draw a series of approximately 20 squares measuring 3 x 3cm (1⅛ x 1⅛in), then cut out the squares using a pair of scissors. Feel free to use whatever scraps you have to hand. Coloured card is best – but a cereal box will do. Here we used some hand-dyed coloured card. (See page 26 for more information on hand dyeing.)

2. Repeat this process for as many other basic geometric shapes as you like: diamonds, rectangles, equilateral triangles, right-angled triangles, circles and half circles are particularly useful. In addition, feel free to try any other shapes you can think of, but make sure you cut all the shapes to similar proportions. For example, if your squares are 3 x 3cm (1⅛ x 1⅛in), then make sure your circles have a diameter of 3cm (1⅛in) and your right-angled triangles have two sides measuring 3cm (1⅛in), this will ensure that when you start playing around with pattern design your shapes will fit together neatly to make regular repeats.

3. Next, cut out two additional sets of geometric shapes to a half and a quarter of the size of your original set. These additional sizes will give you plenty of options to play around with.

4. Place your shapes on a plain background, a tabletop or large coloured sheet of card are fine, and see how many ways you can combine your set of geometric shapes to form a series of patterns. Once you've got the hang of it try creating more complex patterns by taking inspiration from Victorian and Islamic tile designs.

5. Record the pattern designs you come up with along the way, either by photographing or sketching your arrangements.

6. While you play with the patterns, ensure you explore the three key ways of creating repeats: regular repeats, where all the shapes line up in a grid format; half-drop repeats, where your second line of shapes drops out of alignment with the first line maintaining an overlap; and multiple-drop repeats, where your second line of shapes drops out of alignment with no overlap.

7. Once you've designed a pattern you like, turn it into wrapping paper or wallpaper by following the instructions in projects 18 (see page 86) or 19 (see page 94).

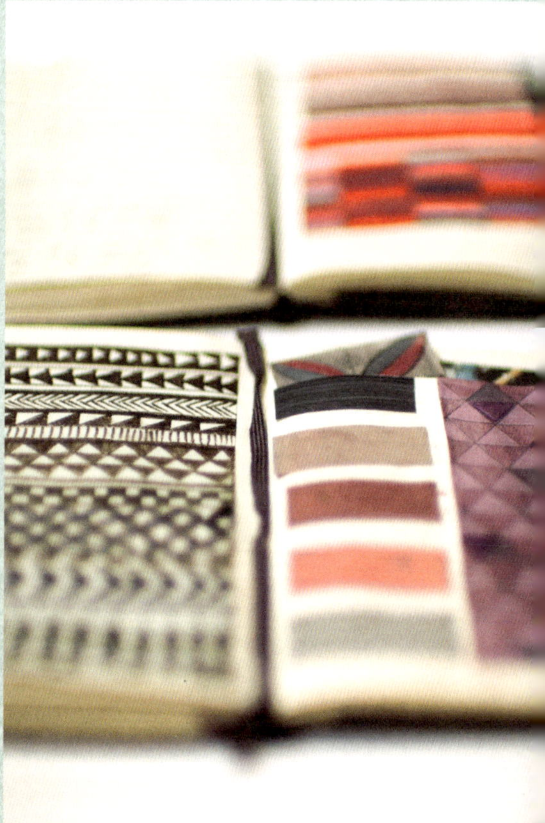

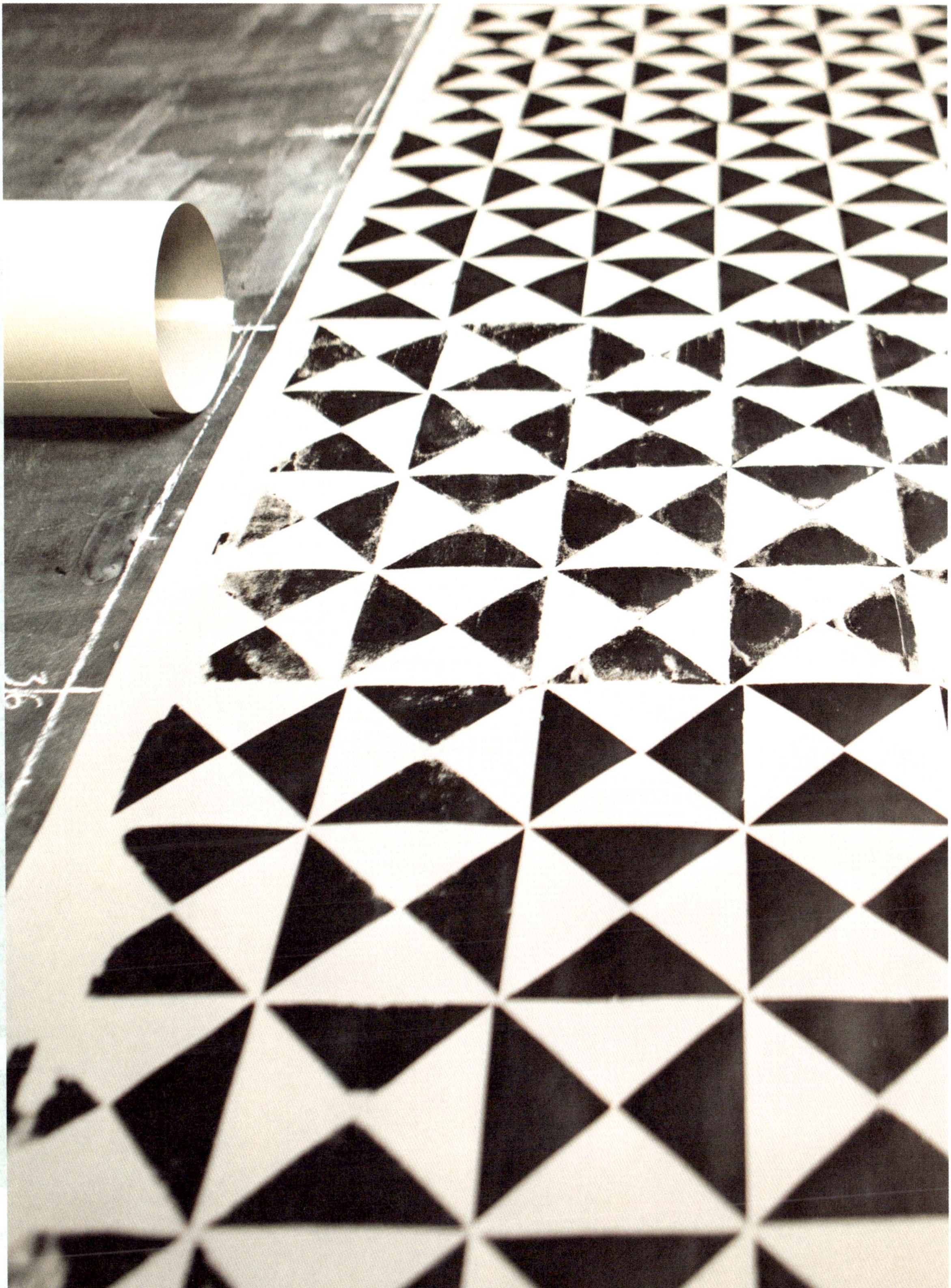

16

WHAT YOU NEED

- A collection of things you want to turn into a pattern design
- Piece of paper
- Pencil
- Eraser

P·A·T·T·E·R·N D·E·S·I·G·N

VARIATIONS ON A THEME

× HERE'S A SECOND WAY TO DEVELOP YOUR OWN PATTERN DESIGNS. ONCE YOU'VE DESIGNED YOUR BASIC BLOCK IT CAN BE USED AS THE BASIS FOR A SCREEN-PRINTED POSTER DESIGN OR TURNED INTO A REPEATING PATTERN AND MADE INTO WALLPAPER.

1. Put together a collection of 5–8 different types of the same thing – for example, here we've collected leaves. You can basically use anything you like but it's a good idea to make sure that the items are all a similar size.

2. Lay your collection out on a flat surface and play around with different arrangements until you come up with an order you like more than any other.

3. Take a piece of paper and make a line drawing of your arrangement. Begin by getting the rough details down, including the general shapes that make up each of the items. Make sure that you accurately represent the distance between each item, and then, once the basics are in place, start to add the details.

4. You now have a basic pattern design ready for printing – just follow the instructions in projects 18 (see page 86) or 19 (see page 94).

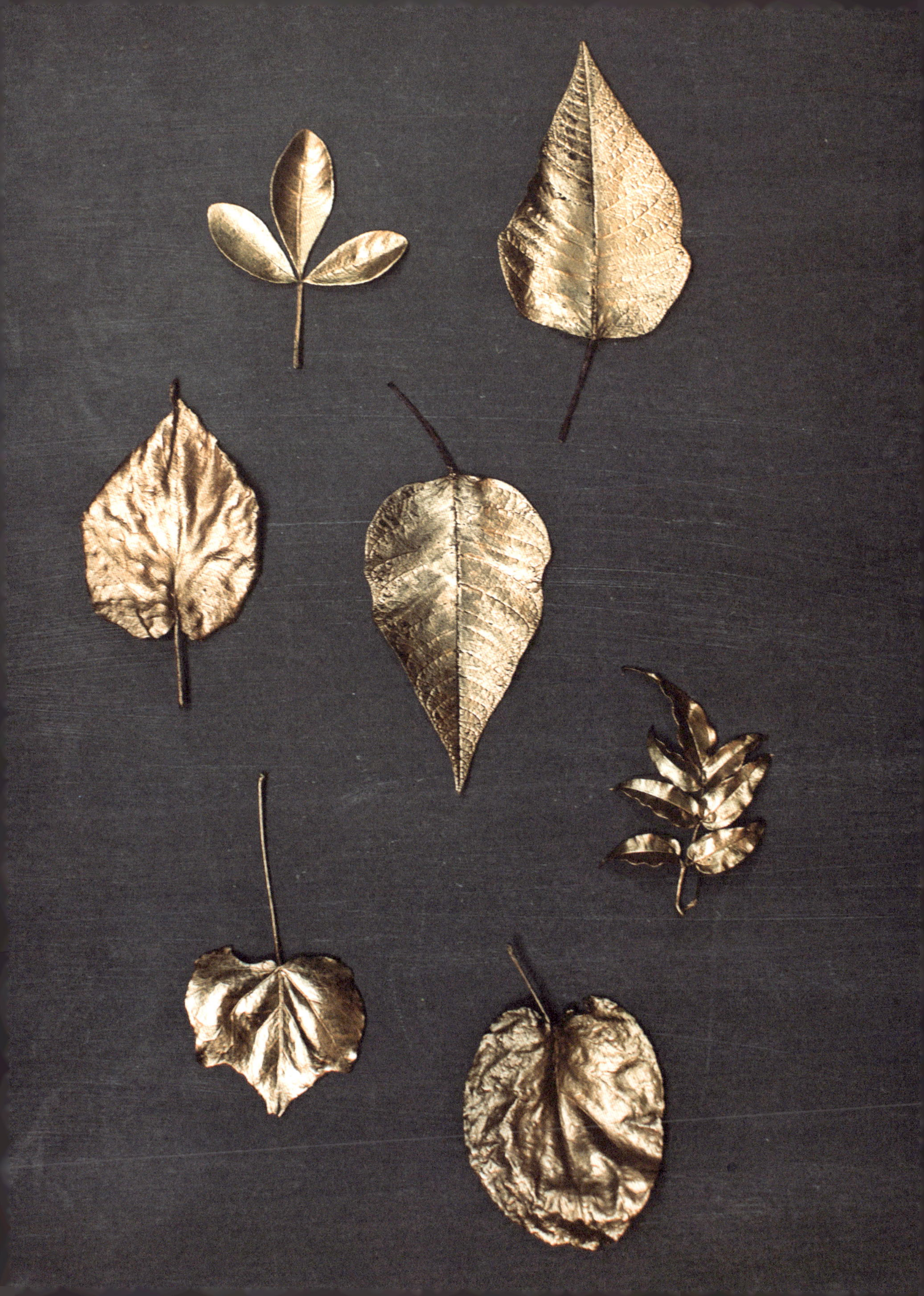

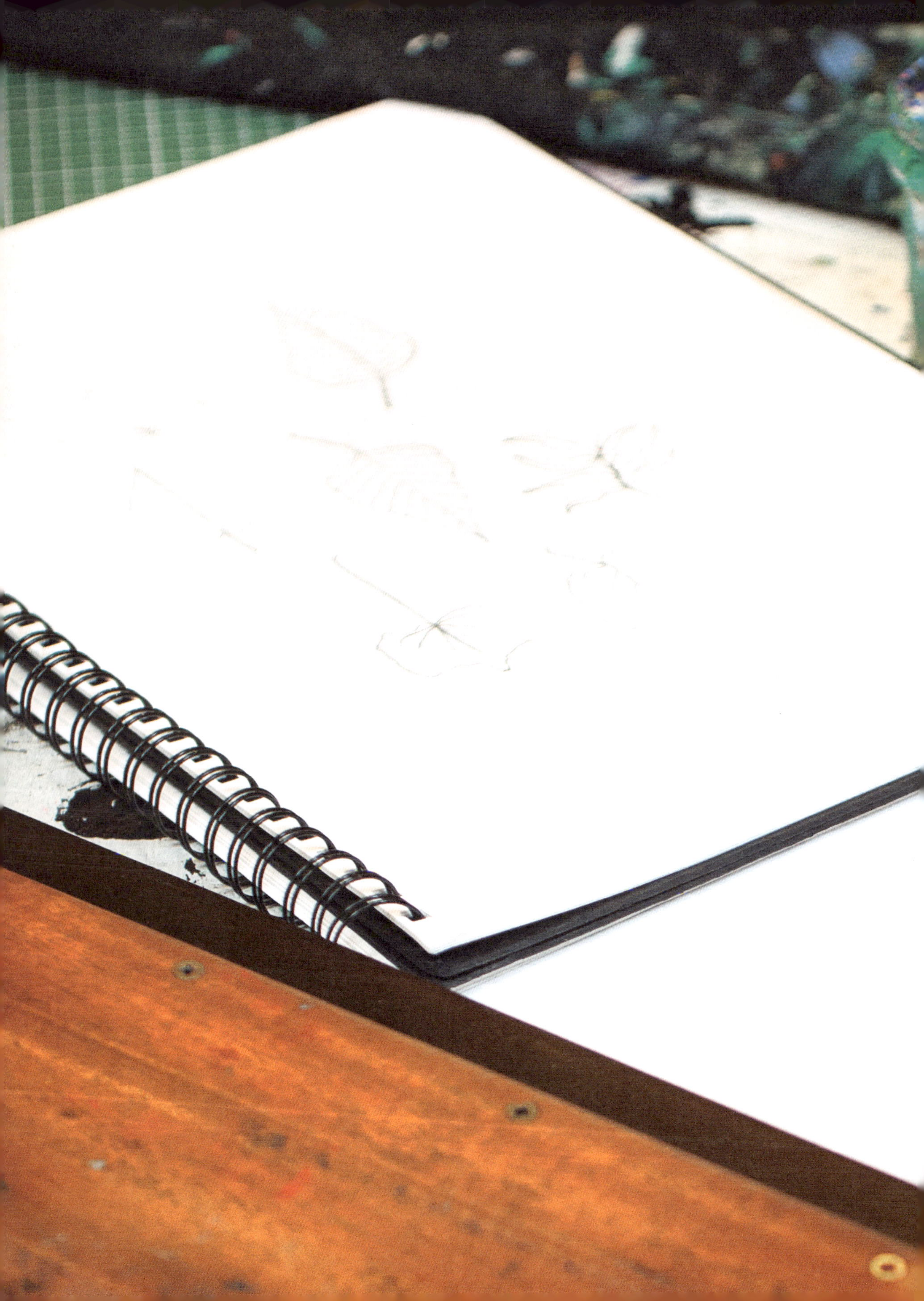

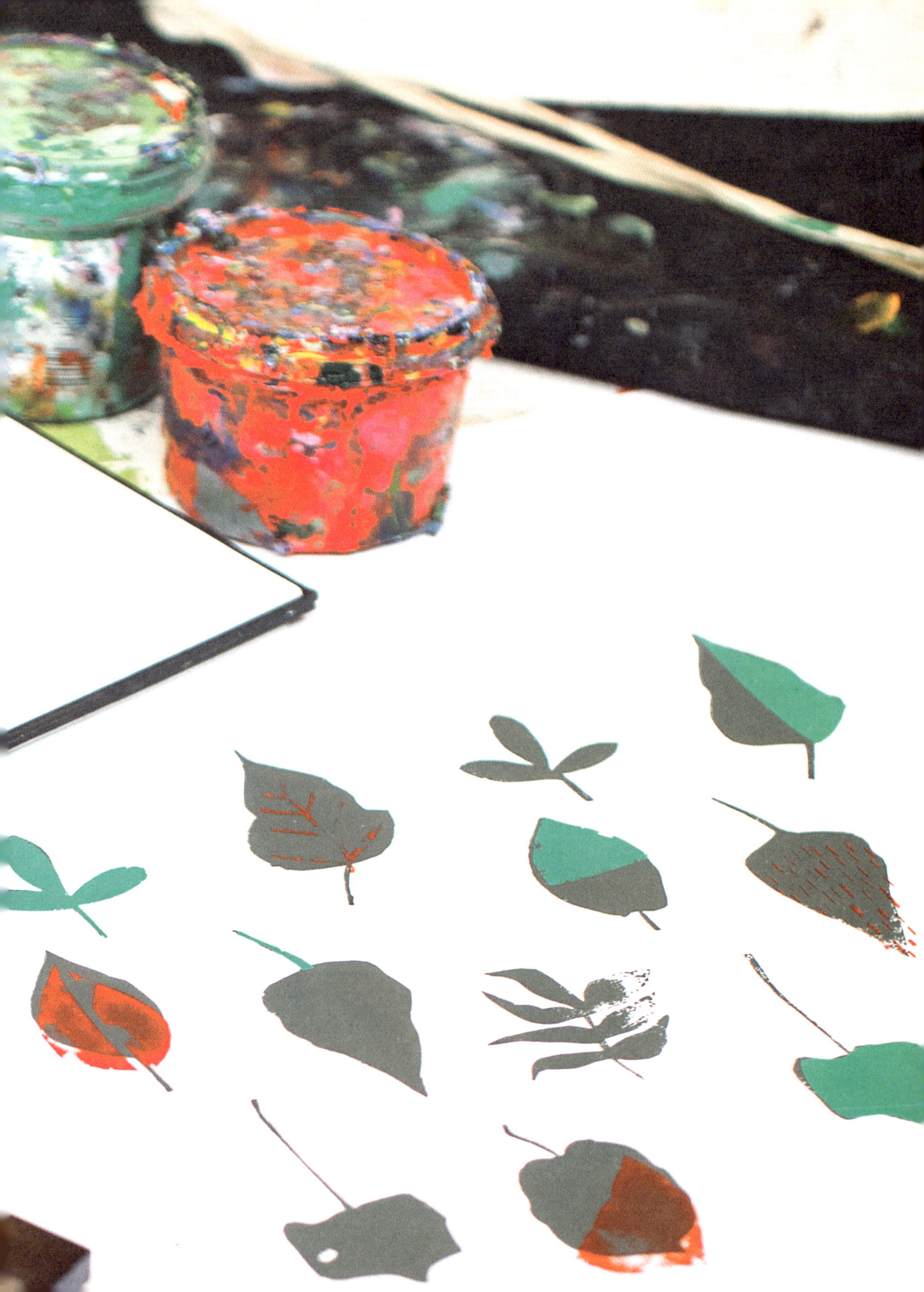

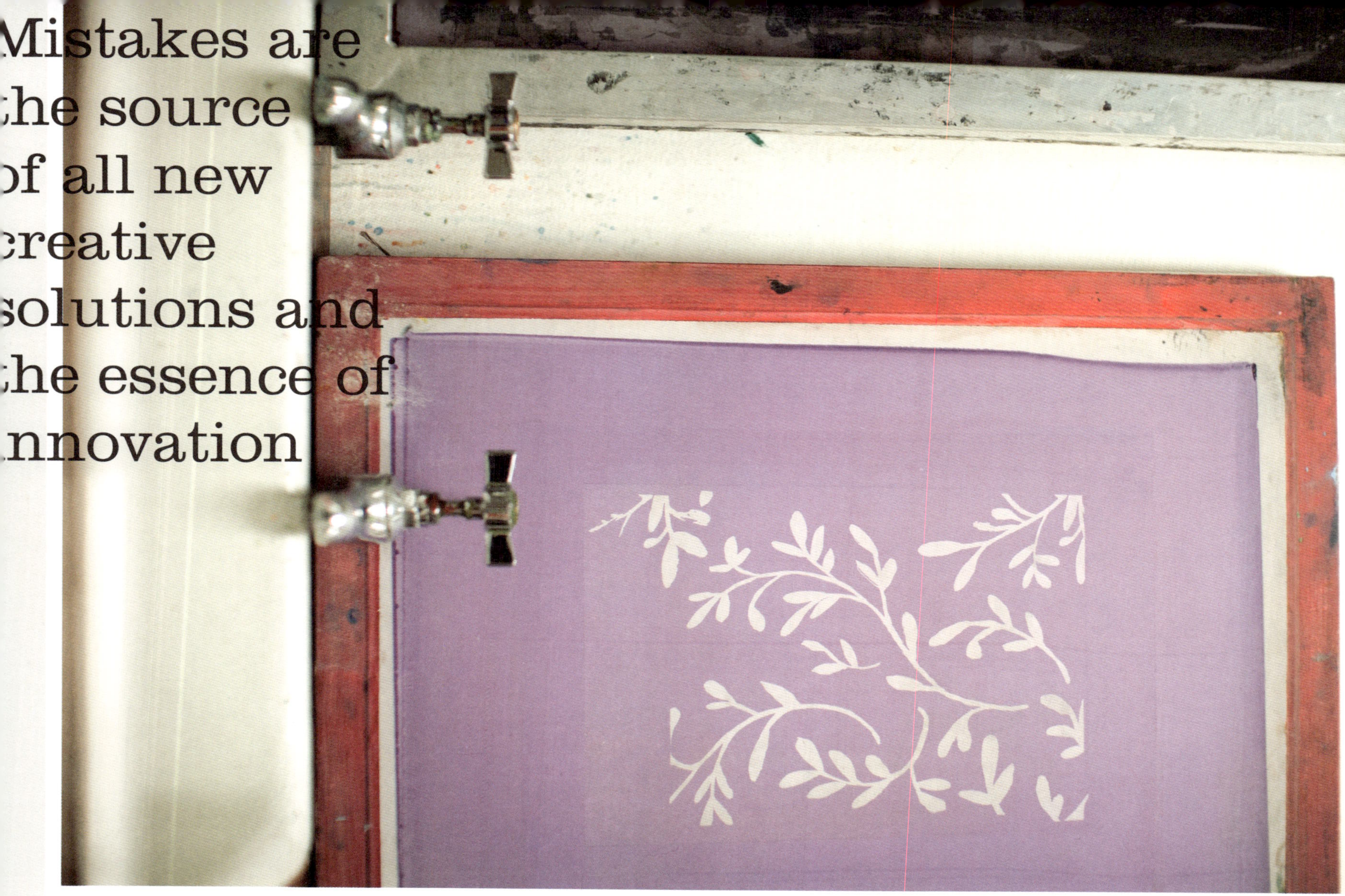

Mistakes are
the source
of all new
creative
solutions and
the essence of
innovation

17

R·E·P·E·A·T·I·N·G P·A·T·T·E·R·N·S

WHAT YOU NEED

- Paper
- Pencil
- Paint
- Scissors
- Clear sticky tape

e h 2 £ 5 ↓

× DEVELOP YOUR OWN DECORATIVE DESIGNS BY LEARNING HOW TO MAKE PERFECTLY REPEATING PATTERNS. THE EYE ENJOYS SYMMETRY AND SIMILARITY SO FOLLOW THESE SIMPLE STEPS TO CREATE BASIC PRINTING BLOCKS THAT LOOK PHENOMENAL IN REPEAT.

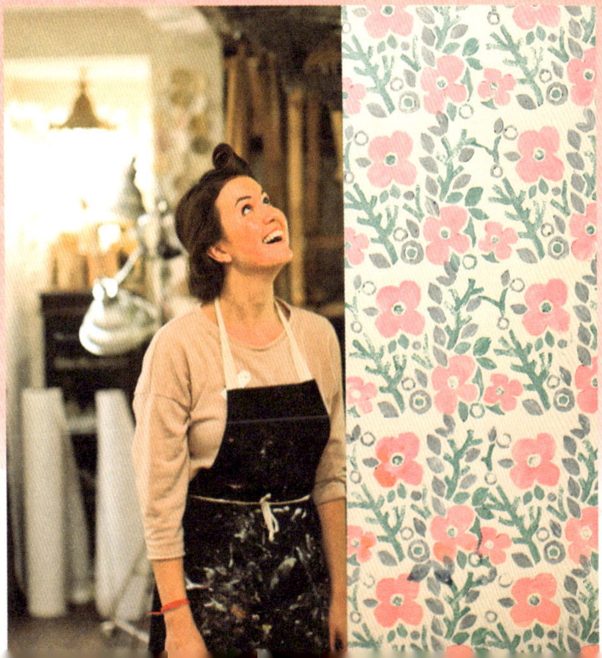

Innovation can't be forced, let ideas emerge naturally as you play

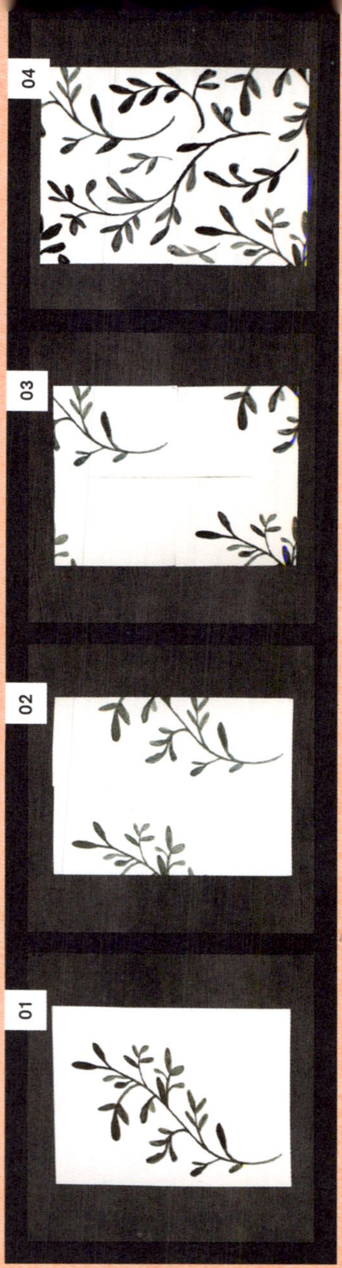

1. Draw a design in the centre of your paper. It doesn't need to be complicated – keep it simple.

2. Carefully cut the sheet of paper in half vertically, making sure you keep the cut as straight as possible. Use a guillotine if you have access to one. Next, rearrange the two halves of the paper so that the centre of the design is now on the outer edges. Stick the two halves back together neatly with tape.

3. Repeat the process, this time cutting the sheet in half horizontally, and then sticking it back together again with the centre of the design on the outside.

4. Now fill in the gaps by adding extra hand-drawn elements to complete your design. You now have a basic tile that can be printed to form a repeating pattern. Turn this into a block or a stencil and use it to block- or screen-print your own wallpaper or wrapping paper.

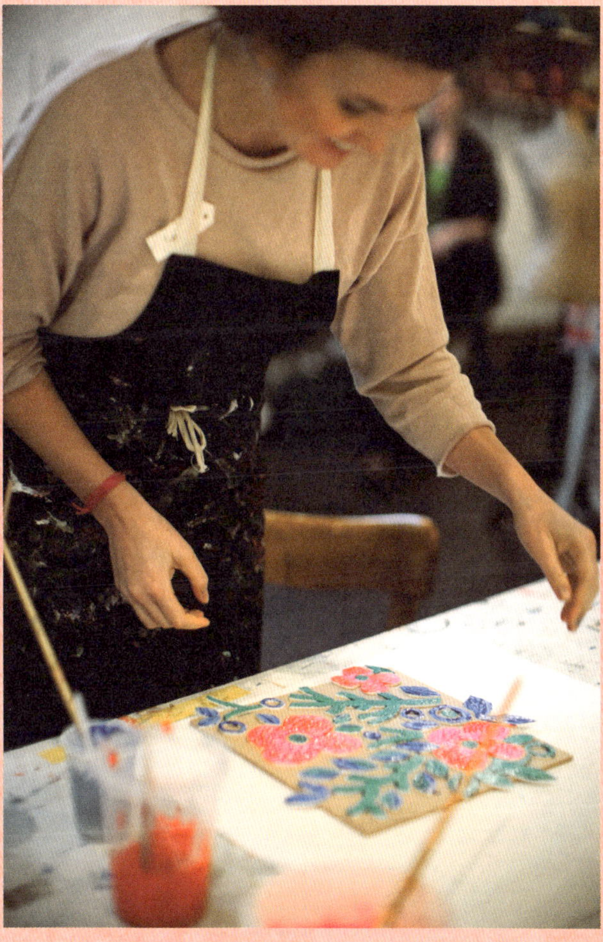

18

B·L·O·C·K-P·R·I·N·T·E·D W·A·L·L·P·A·P·E·R

× MAKING YOUR OWN WALLPAPER IS SURPRISINGLY SIMPLE. WHETHER YOU WANT TO REINVIGORATE YOUR ROOM OR FINISH A FEATURE WALL IN A DAY – ALL IT TAKES IS A LITTLE BIT OF KNOW-HOW. SO GET READY TO CUT YOUR OWN PRINTING BLOCK AND YOU'LL BE TRANSFORMING YOUR PLAIN WHITE WALLS INTO ELEGANT INTERIORS IN NO TIME.

m

h 5-10

£ 50 ↓

WHAT YOU NEED

- 2 x 170cm (5½ft) lengths of lining paper
- 2 acrylic paint colours (System 3, Farrow & Ball sample pots or any other acrylic-based paint is fine)
- A tub of System 3 print medium
- 1 x A4 polystyrene sheet
- 1 x 3mm (⅛in) A4 MDF board
- Pencil
- Biro
- Eraser
- A4 plain paper
- Also needed: plastic pots to mix the paint in, paint brushes, masking tape, ruler, craft knife

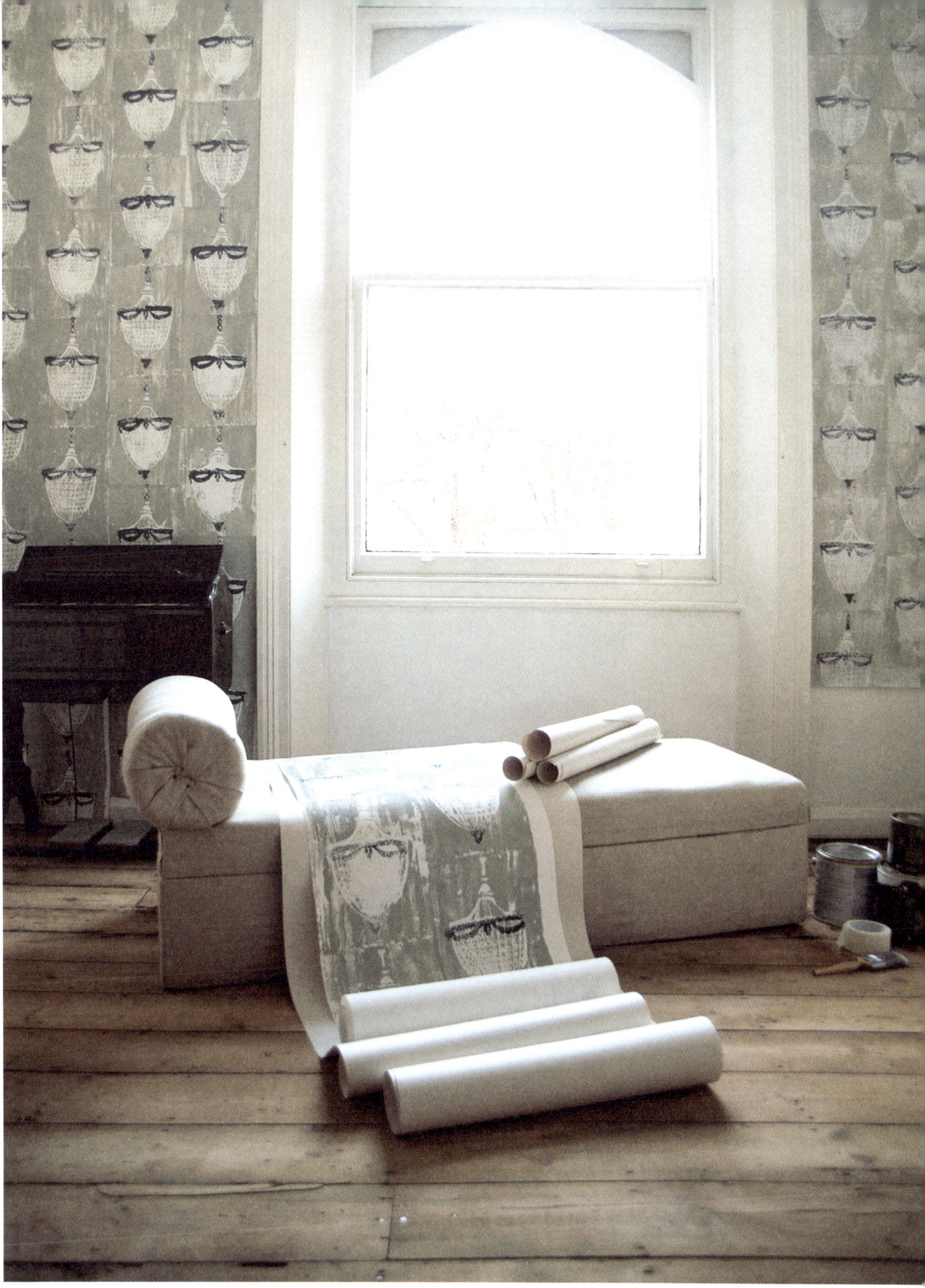

1. Make a rough still-life sketch of your chosen subject or compose a drawing based on a photograph or found image. Don't worry if your drawing is not perfect, this is about capturing character through the marks you make on the paper. This initial sketch will end up as a silhouette so it's the shape that matters most. Don't forget to pay close attention to perspective and the finer details – these may end up being the key components that make your design stand out.

2. Simplify your drawing, eliminating unnecessary details with shading. Foreground essential elements by painting them a brighter colour and darken structural lines to highlight the key shapes. Divide the drawing into positive and negative space by imagining how the design will look when printed – positive space is where paint will be transferred from the block onto the paper, negative space is what will remain white.

3. Place your drawing onto the sheet of polystyrene. Trace around the outside of your design, making an impression on the polystyrene underneath. Remove the paper and draw around the imprint with a biro to create a strong guideline ready for cutting. Cut out the design using a craft knife. For finer detail use a biro to make an impression on the polystyrene.

4. Stick the polystyrene templates onto an MDF board to create your blocks.

5. Using a paint brush, apply the acrylic paint to your first printing block. You can be as rough and ready or as precise as you like. We used a freehand approach so the finished wallpaper would pick up the texture of the brush strokes, but it's also fine to be really precise.

6. Line up your block with the edge of your wallpaper, place the block face down and apply pressure. After approximately 10 seconds peel the block away, reapply the paint to the block and repeat the printing process. It's a good idea to start with a test print so you know how much paint to apply and what kind of pressure you need to use.

7. To create a half-drop repeat, begin your second line of printing by lining up your block with the middle of the first print. Once you have printed the whole of your 3m (10ft) sheet it's time to add the details, using the smaller block and your secondary colour to print.

8. Trim off any excess paper and your designs will be ready to hang on the wall.

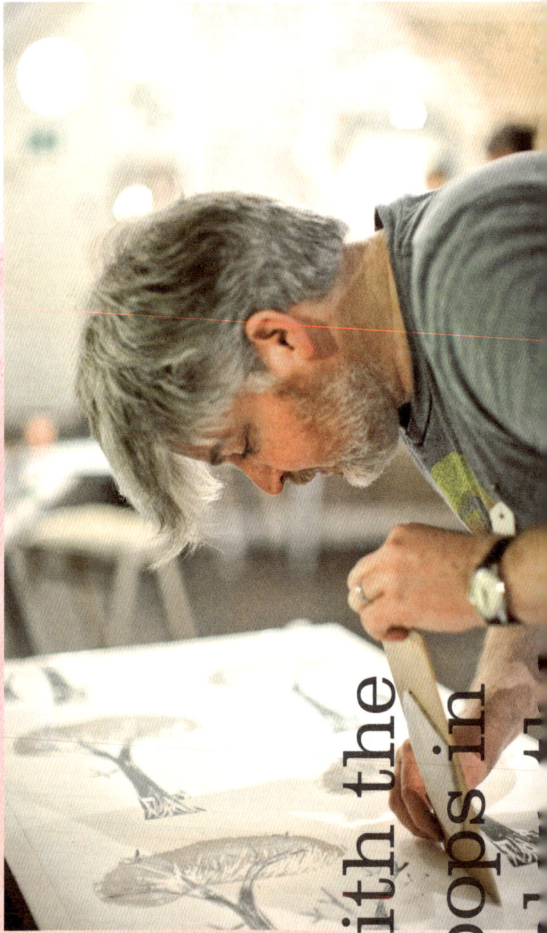

Don't just go with the
first idea that pops in

like and discard the bits
you don’t

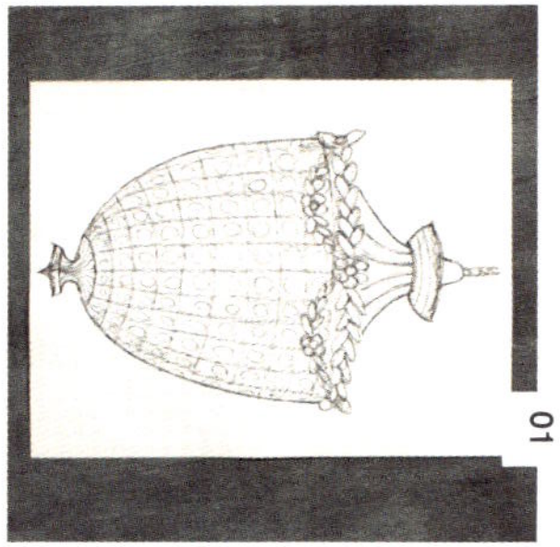
01

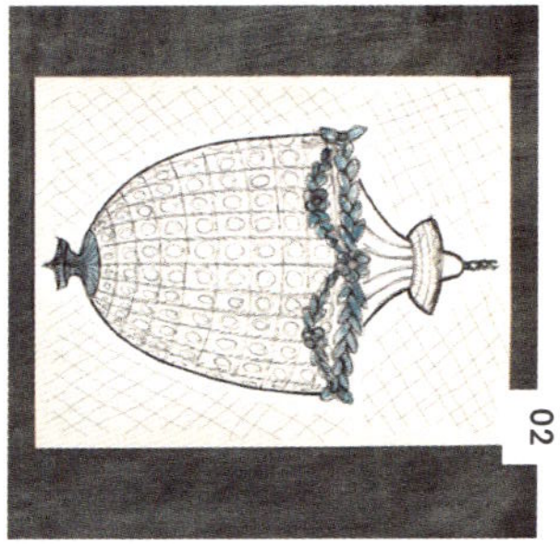
02

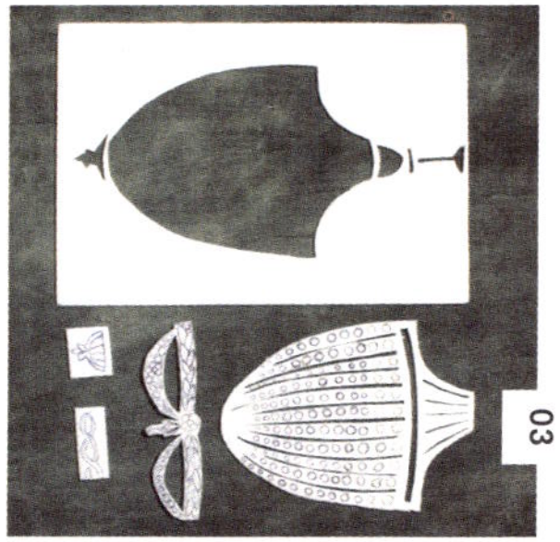
03

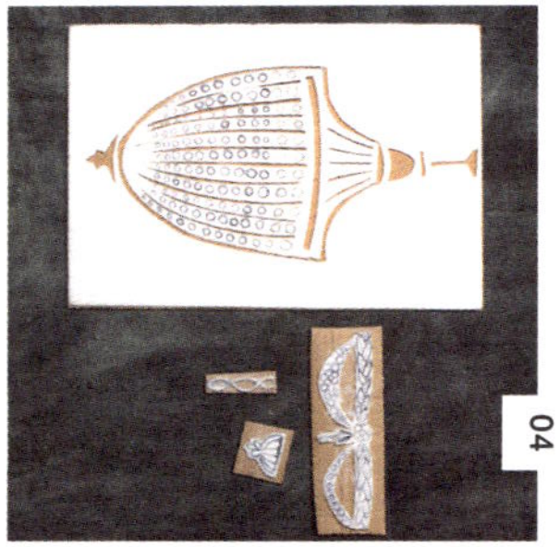
04

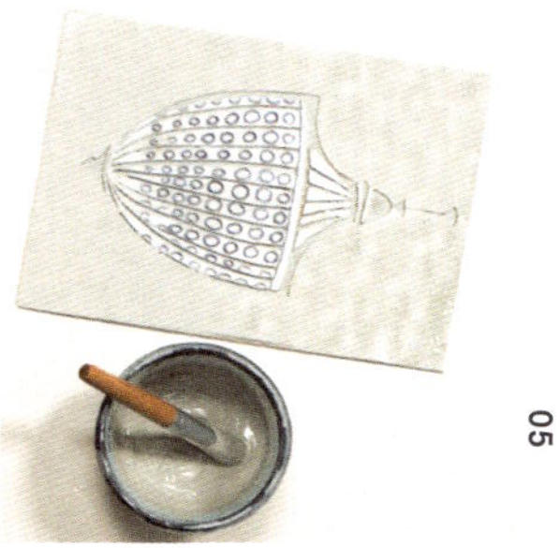
05

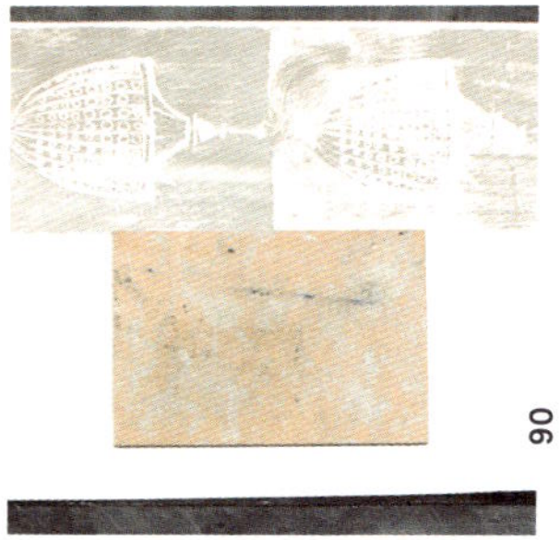
06

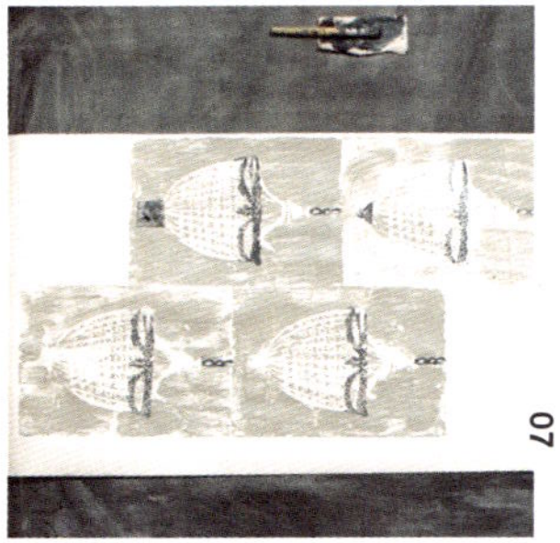
07

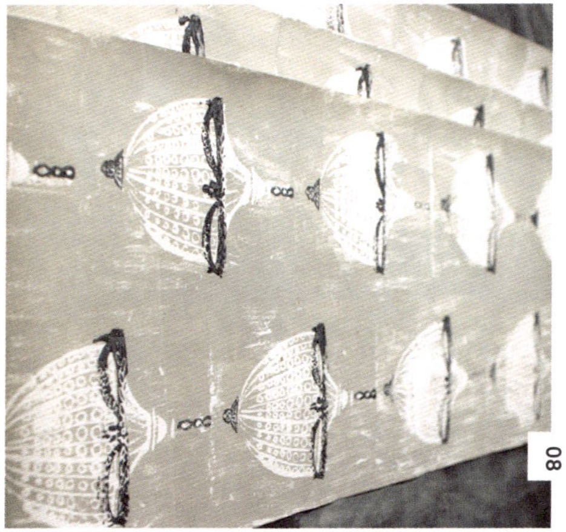
08

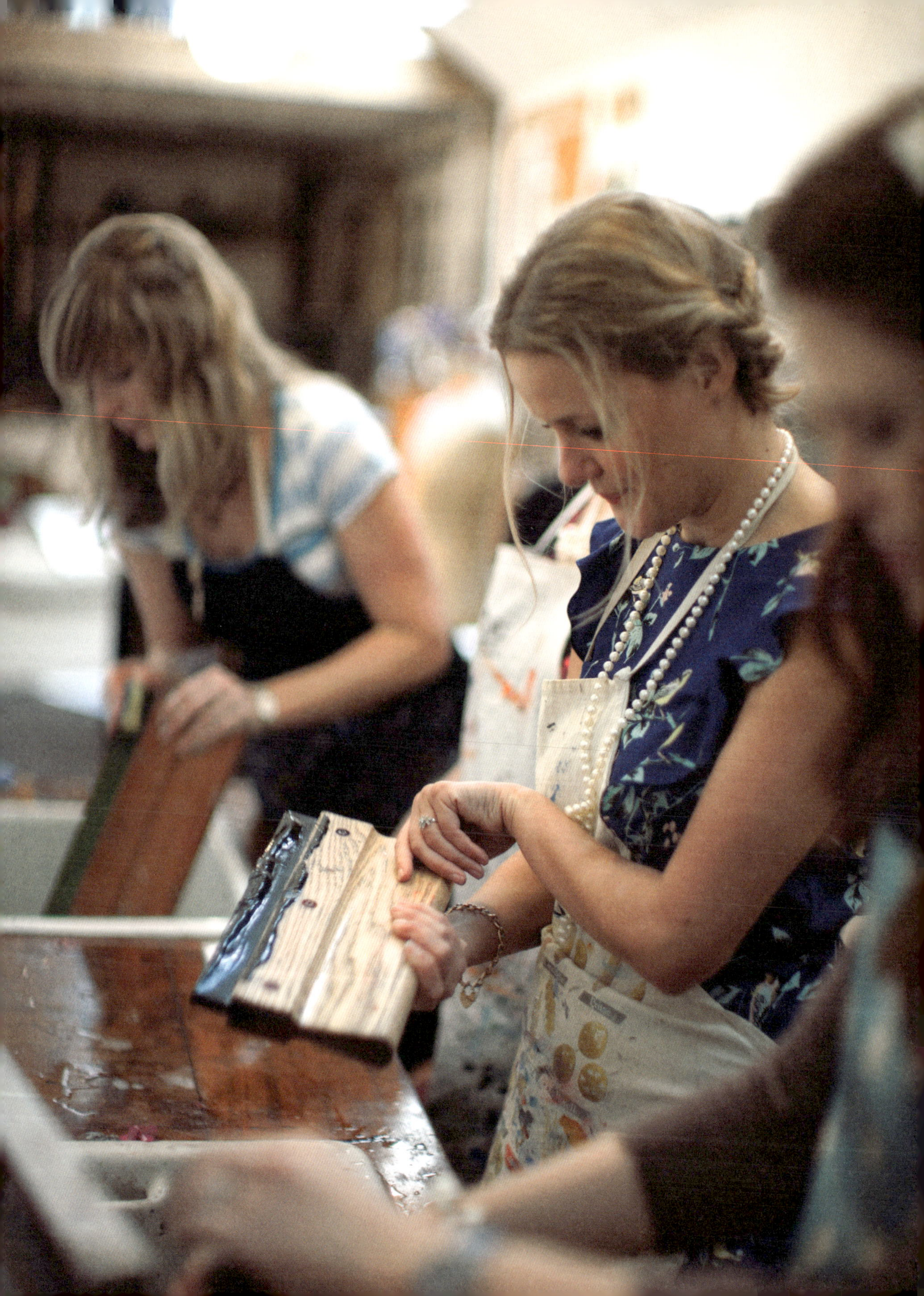

BLOCK-PRINTING vs SCREEN-PRINTING

× ALTHOUGH THERE ARE MANY DIFFERENT WAYS TO PRODUCE BEAUTIFUL WALLPAPER BY HAND, IN THIS BOOK WE'VE CHOSEN TO FOCUS ON BLOCK-PRINTING AND DIY SCREEN-PRINTING. THESE TWO METHODS ARE FUN AND SIMPLE AND CAN PRODUCE STUNNING RESULTS WITH MINIMAL EFFORT AND EXPENSE.

× EACH METHOD OF PRINTING HAS SLIGHTLY DIFFERENT ADVANTAGES. BLOCK-PRINTING IS EASY TO SET UP AND IS FANTASTIC FOR ADDING WARMTH AND TEXTURE TO QUIRKY INTERIORS. CONVERSELY, SCREEN-PRINTING IS A LITTLE TRICKIER TO SET UP, BUT WORKS WELL FOR GEOMETRIC PATTERNS, AND IS SUPER-FAST ONCE YOU GET PRINTING. THE TABLE BELOW LISTS THE SPECIFICS OF EACH METHOD – READ IT THROUGH AND DECIDE WHICH TECHNIQUE WILL WORK BEST FOR YOU.

BLOCK-PRINTING WALLPAPER

× Easy to set up (1–2 hours)
× Can be printed intuitively
× Great for adding a rich, painterly texture to your interiors
× Can be printed alone
× Slow to print (3 hours plus)

SCREEN-PRINTING WALLPAPER

× Slow to set up (3 hours plus)
× Requires precision
× Creates sharp blocks of flat colour, perfect for geometric repeats
× Requires 2 or 3 people
× Fast to print (1 hour)

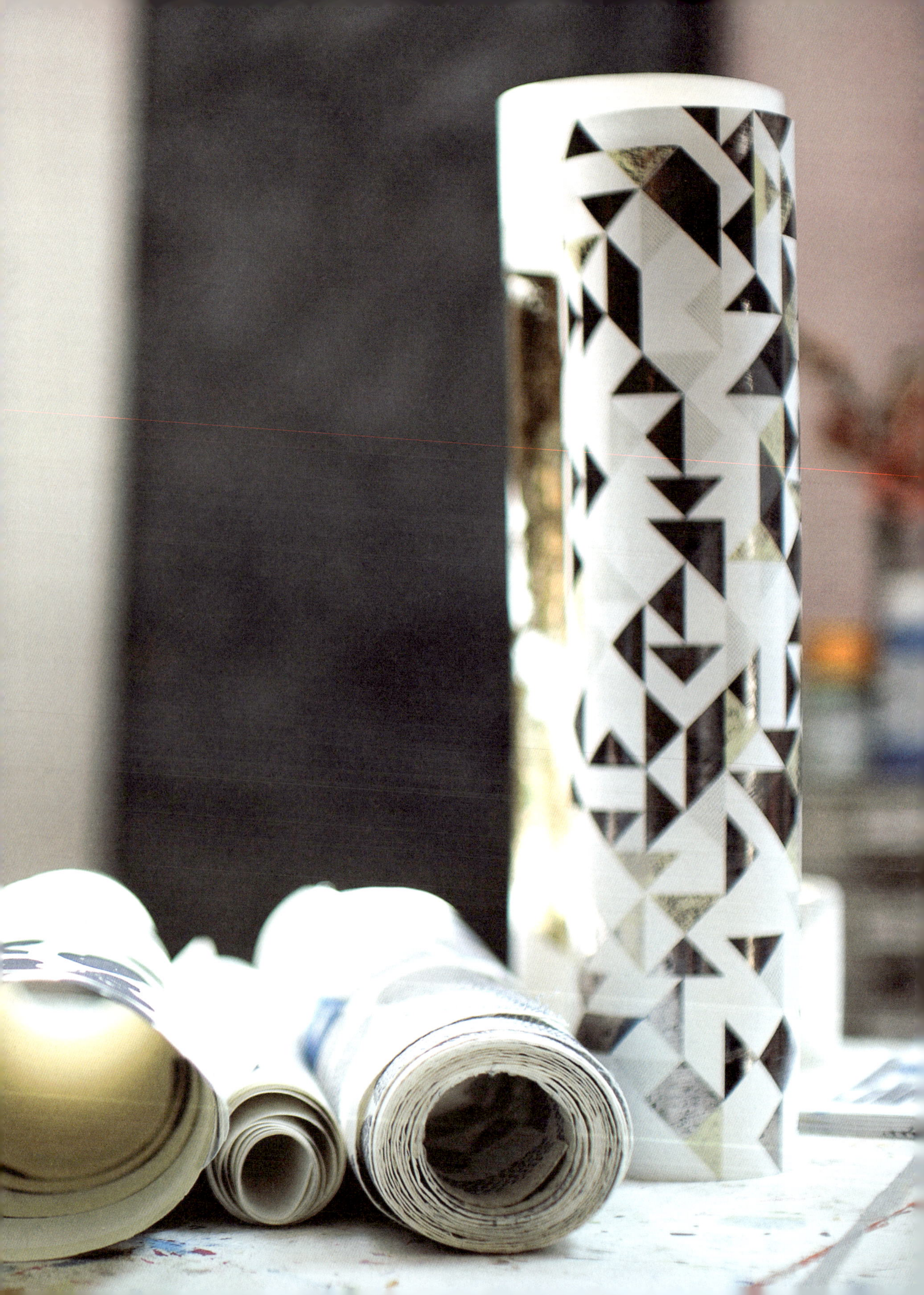

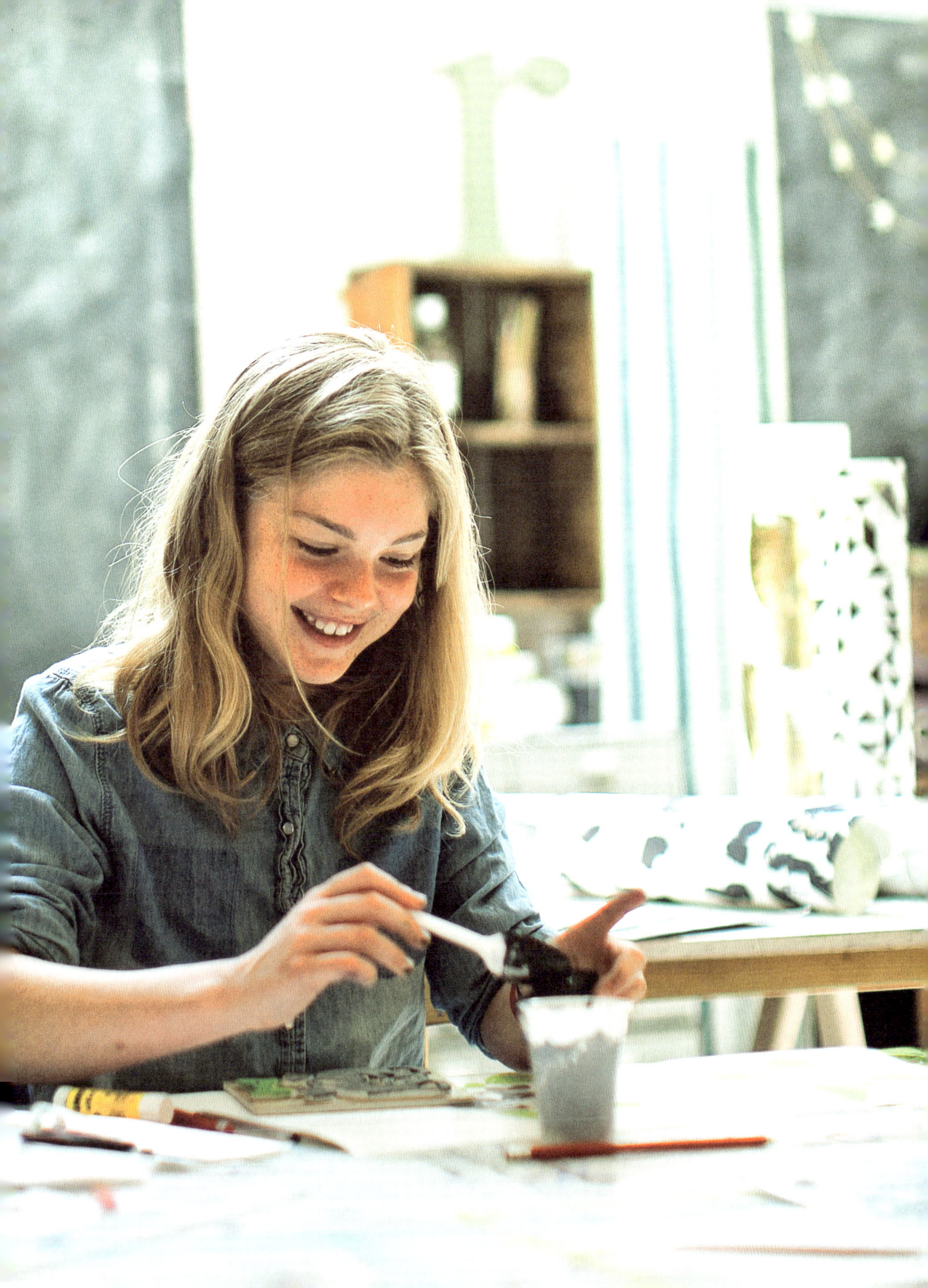

S·C·R·E·E·N-P·R·I·N·T·E·D W·A·L·L·P·A·P·E·R

× THIS PROJECT IS A LITTLE TRICKIER THAN SOME OF THE OTHERS IN THE BOOK, BUT IF YOU FOLLOW THE INSTRUCTIONS CAREFULLY AND ARE PREPARED TO MAKE A FEW MISTAKES FIRST TIME ROUND, YOU'LL BE SCREEN-PRINTING STUNNING WALLPAPER IN NO TIME. THE MAIN CHALLENGE WHEN CREATING FORMAL REPEATING PATTERNS IS GETTING THE MEASUREMENTS RIGHT, SO THAT YOUR BASIC DESIGN BLOCK ALIGNS NEATLY TO CREATE A CONTINUOUS REPEAT. THIS PART IS LESS ABOUT ART AND MORE ABOUT BASIC MATHS. SO, IN THIS EXAMPLE, WE'VE DONE THE CALCULATIONS FOR YOU, BASED ON THE FACT THAT WALLPAPER AND SILK SCREENS COME IN STANDARD SIZES. JUST FOLLOW THE MEASUREMENTS BELOW AND YOUR PRINTS SHOULD MATCH UP NICELY.

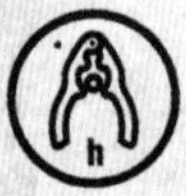

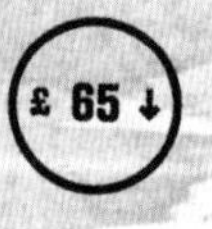

WHAT YOU NEED

- A2 cartridge paper or card
- A1 newsprint
- Marker pen, fine-tipped pen and pencil
- Ruler
- 48 x 61cm (19 x 24in) silk screen
- Kitchen table or trestle table
- Plastic tablecloth
- 2 x 170cm (5½ft) lengths of lining paper
- Small tin of acrylic or high-quality emulsion paint
- Screen-print textile medium
- Small foam roller
- Squeegee
- 2 or 3 people
- Also needed: craft knife or scissors, brown tape, masking tape, cardboard, plastic pot and spoon, hairdryer

THIS PROJECT HAS THREE STAGES

Design (1–3 hours): Generate a geometric pattern (see page 74).
Preparing the screen (2 hours): Cut out the paper stencil and set up the screen.
Printing (1 hour): Apply the base colour and print the design.

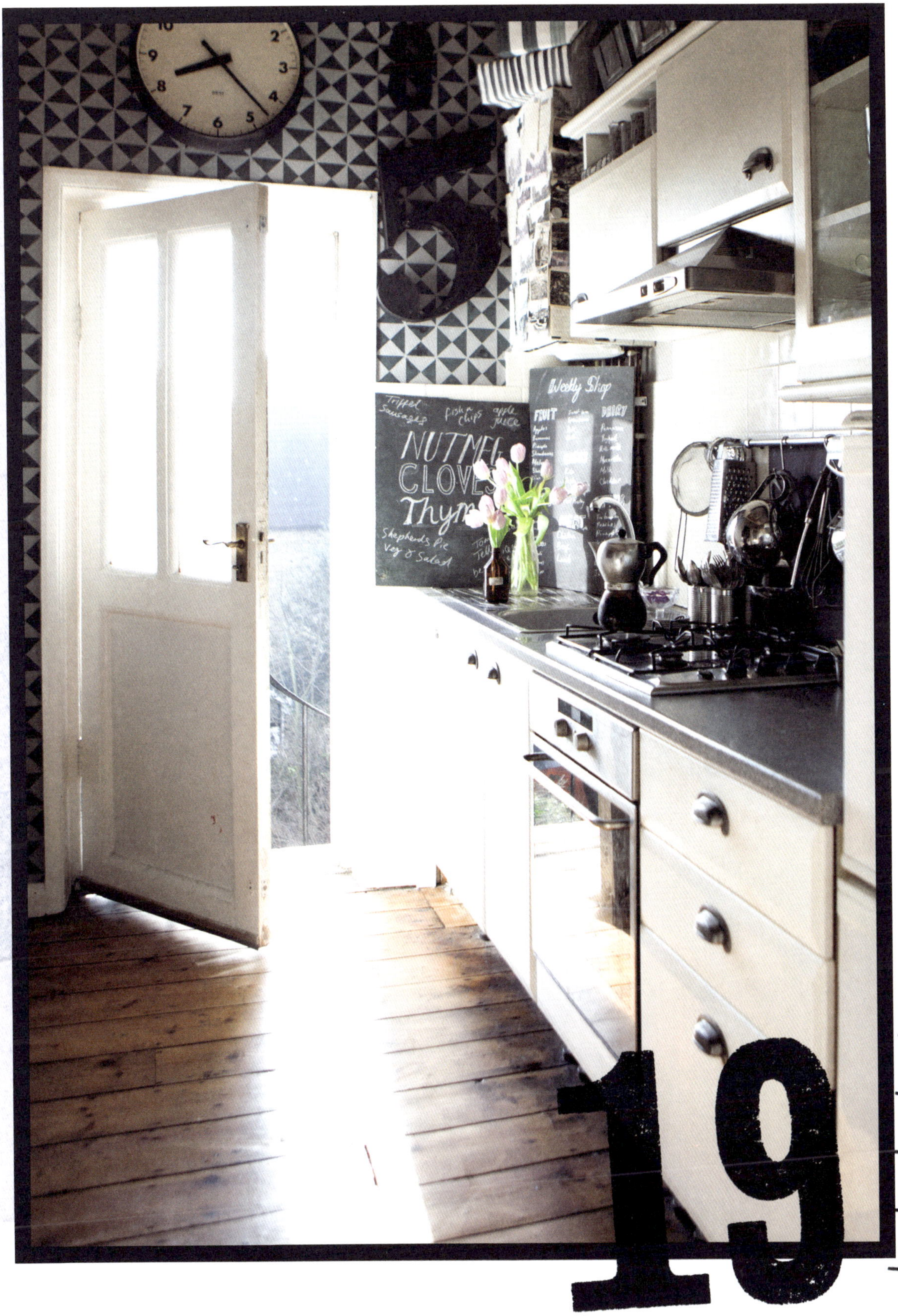
Weekly Shop
FRUIT
DAIRY
fish n chips
apple juice
Shepherds Pie
Veg & Salad

19

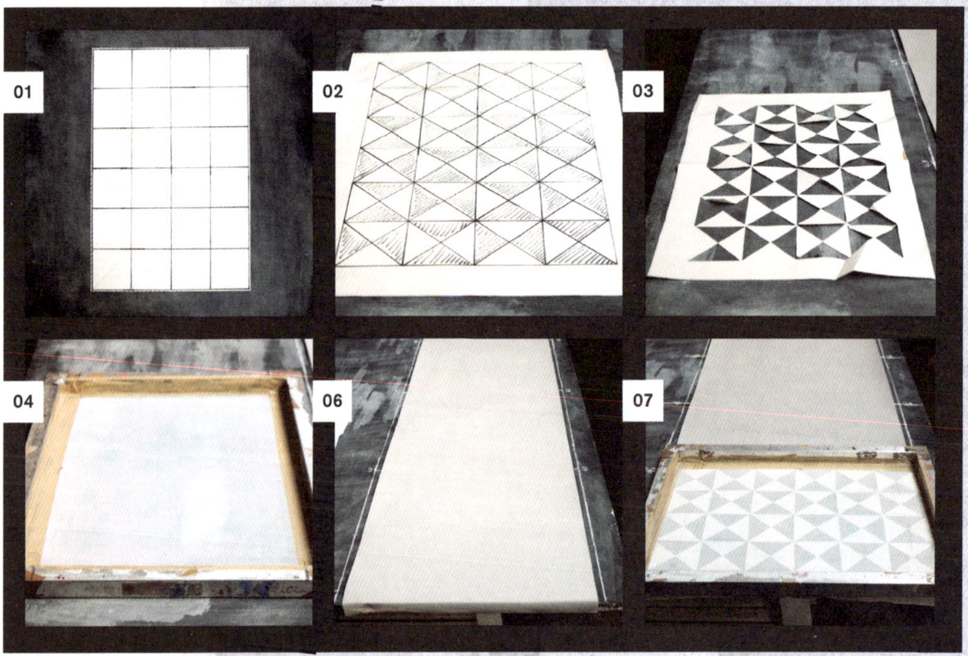
01
02
03
04
06
07

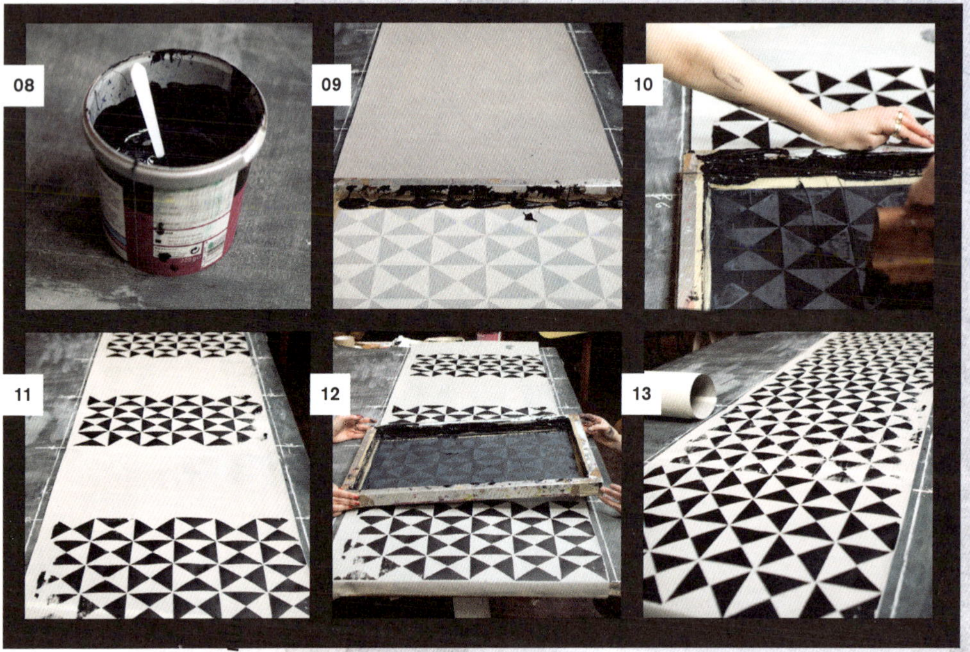
08
09
10
11
12
13

PREPARING THE SCREEN

1. Draw a 4 x 6 square grid on an A2 piece of cartridge paper or card. Each square should measure 9 x 9cm (3½ x 3½in), with the overall grid measuring 36 x 54cm (14⅛ x 21¼in). Draw the main outlines of the grid in a thick marker pen and then add diagonal guidelines with a fine-tipped pen. This grid can be used as a design grid each time you are preparing a screen to make geometric wallpaper.

2. Take the A1 newsprint and lay it on the grid. Plot your design on the newsprint in pencil. The key here is to make sure you think about how the pattern is going to repeat. This means making sure the edges of the pattern will match up to form a continuous design. Play around with a few sketches until you are sure that you understand how the pattern is going to work. It's worth checking this a couple of times just to be on the safe side. Trace out your pattern using a pencil, and then mark the parts of the design that need to be cut away to create your stencil.

3. Cut out your stencil and then trim the edges to cut away the surplus newsprint.

4. Next, it's time to get your screen set up. Place the screen mesh side down, orientated in the portrait position. In each corner, measure 3cm (1⅛in) horizontally in from the external edge of the metal frame. Use a marker pen to draw four perpendicular lines at the 3cm (1⅛in) mark. Next, create a gutter along the long vertical edges where the paint is going to collect when printing. Halfway up the vertical edges, measure in 3cm (1⅛in) horizontally from the outside edge, and make a small mark, this time on the mesh. Now cut a length of brown tape and line it up with the mark on the mesh. The brown tape should be in alignment with the four lines in each corner and should fold up on the inside of the metal screen. Fill any gaps with small pieces of tape – the aim is to seal the screen so that the brown tape forms a waterproof gutter.

5. Finally, turn your screen over and cut out four small squares of cardboard to be placed in the corners of screen. Stick them down with brown tape so that they are held securely in place. These allow the screen to sit slightly away from the paper when printing.

PRINTING

6. Spread out a plastic tablecloth on your tabletop and lay out your sheets of lining paper as shown in image 06. Using a small foam roller, apply your base colour to the paper. If your paint has a high level of pigment, only one coat should be necessary, but two will ensure flawless coverage.

7. Place your screen directly over the length of lining paper, making sure you leave an even space of around 2cm (¾in) at either end. Using masking tape, chalk or a pen, draw four sets of marks on the table in line with the four marks you made on the screen. These marks represent the edge of your pattern and will show you where to line up the screen when you start printing. Now repeat the process, making another four sets of marks on the table every 36cm (14⅛in). Label each set 1–5.

8. Take out your plastic pot and spoon and mix the paint to the required colour. Use 1 part textile medium to 1 part paint, adjusting the colour until you have the perfect shade.

9. Position your screen over the first set of marks and place the paper stencil underneath the screen, making sure the stencil is laying flat under the mesh with all edges aligned. You are now ready to start printing.

10. Using the plastic spoon, add a generous amount of paint to the gutter. Allocate one person to hold the screen in place and another to pull the paint across the screen. With the screen firmly in position, hold the squeegee at a 45-degree angle and pull the paint across to the gutter on the other side. Make sure you push down on the squeegee very hard! Repeat this process, pushing the paint backwards and forwards as many times as needed until you feel the paint has registered evenly on the paper.

11. Carefully lift the screen. Don't worry if there are a few spots that haven't printed perfectly, you can always touch these up by hand later on. If you have a third person helping you, ask them to use the hairdryer to dry the printed area while you get on with the next print. Repeat the printing process for blocks 3 and 5.

12. Once you have printed blocks 1, 3 and 5, ensure they are dry before printing 2 and 4. This will help to avoid smudges.

13. Remove the finished printed wallpaper from the table and hang it up to dry, then repeat the same process to print your second sheet.

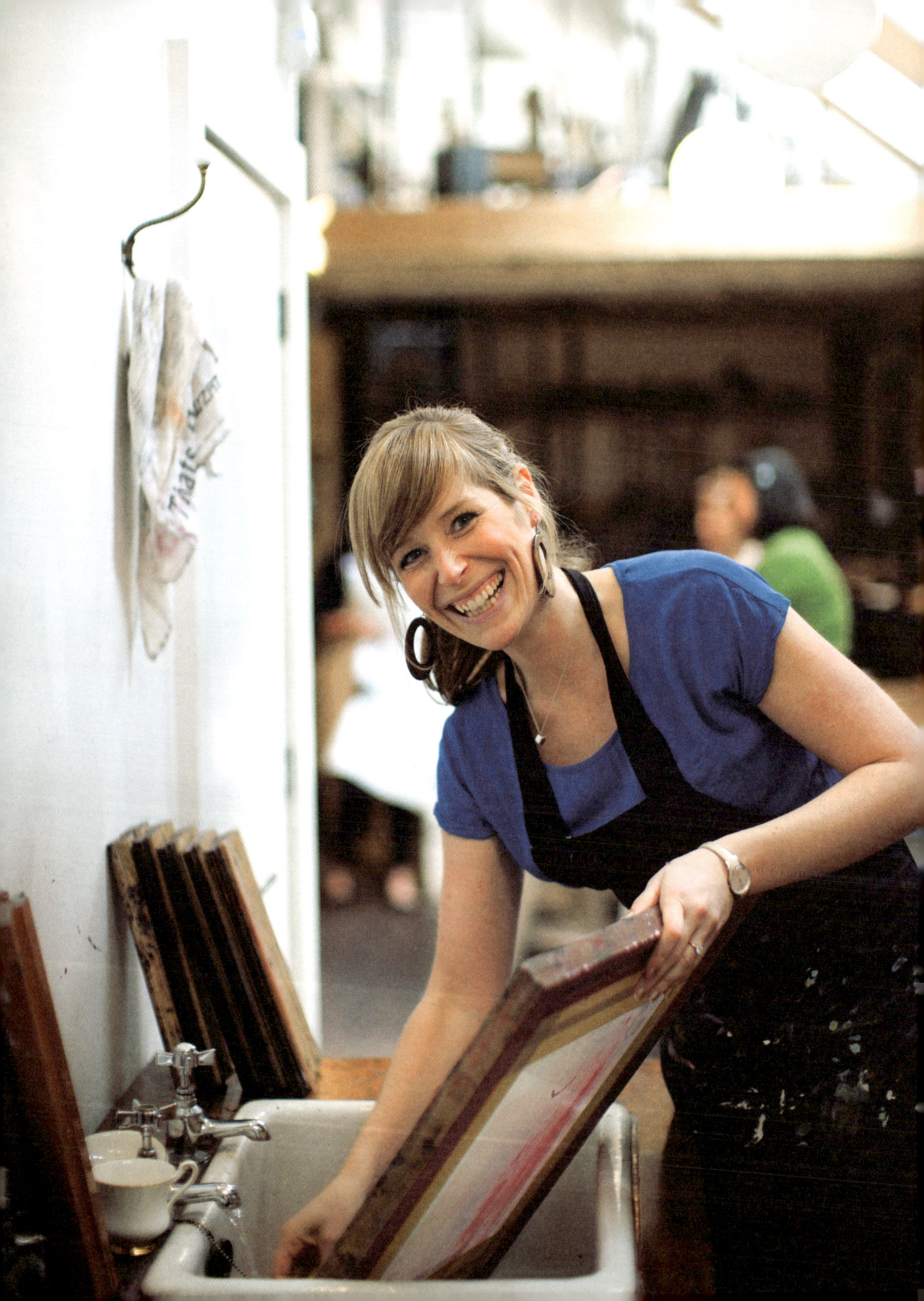

FIVE ESSENTIAL SCREEN-PRINTING TIPS

1 ENSURE YOU USE 1 PART SCREEN-PRINT MEDIUM TO 1 PART ACRYLIC PAINT – IF YOU GET THE PROPORTIONS WRONG, THE PAINT WILL DRY TOO QUICKLY OR TOO SLOWLY.

2 ONCE YOU START PRINTING YOU HAVE AROUND 45 MINUTES BEFORE YOUR SCREEN WILL START TO BLOCK, SO ENSURE YOU ARE PREPARED BEFORE YOU MAKE YOUR FIRST PULL.

3 IT'S A GOOD IDEA TO DO A TEST PRINT BEFORE YOU START PRINTING YOUR WALLPAPER; THIS WILL HELP TO GET THE INK FLOWING EVENLY THROUGH THE MESH FROM THE START.

4 DON'T WORRY IF YOU END UP WITH A FEW AREAS THAT HAVEN'T PRINTED – OR A SPLODGE OR TWO OF INK WHERE YOU DON'T WANT IT – YOU CAN ALWAYS TOUCH IT UP LATER BY HAND.

5 SCREEN-PRINTING IS BASICALLY PLAYING AROUND WITH PAINT, SO BE PREPARED FOR THE INEVITABLE MESS. AND REMEMBER, IF YOU DON'T LIKE WHAT YOU'VE DONE, JUST THROW IT AWAY AND START AGAIN – IT'S ALL PART OF THE LEARNING PROCESS.

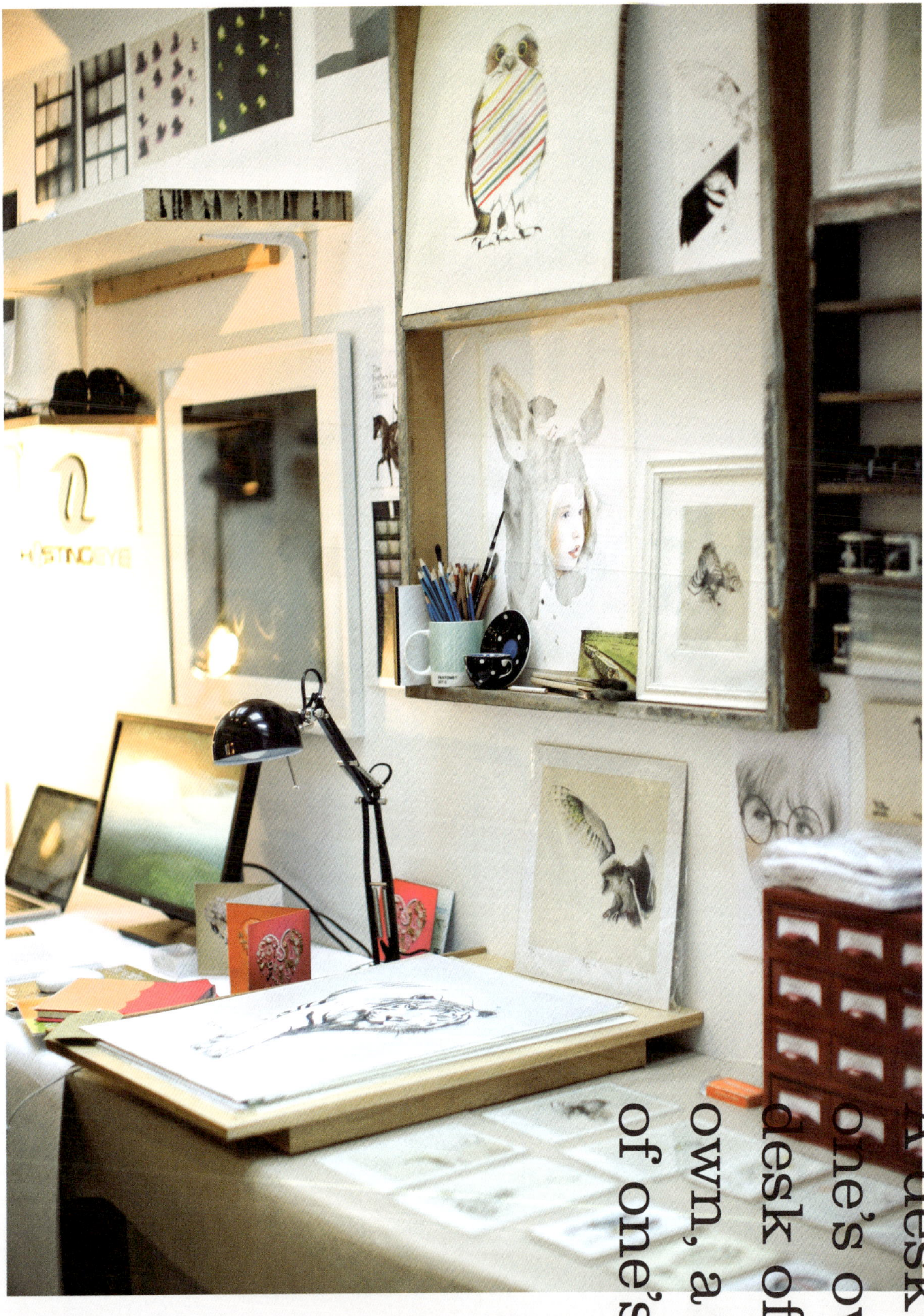

A desk o
one's ow
desk of c
own, a d
of one's c

20

S·E·T U·P Y·O·U·R S·T·U·D·I·O

× MANY OF US DREAM ABOUT HAVING OUR OWN CREATIVE SPACE, BUT WE DON'T ALL HAVE THE LUXURY OF AN ENTIRE ROOM OR STUDIO TO OURSELVES. THIS IS ESPECIALLY TRUE IN BIG CITIES WHERE SPACE IS AT A PREMIUM. AT THE PAPERED PARLOUR WE GET AROUND THIS PROBLEM BY LIMITING OURSELVES TO A DESK AND THEN, WHEN WE NEED TO, WE SPREAD OURSELVES OUT BY MAKING USE OF THE SHARED SPACES. IF YOU WANT TO START DEVELOPING DESIGNS, THEN YOU'RE GOING TO NEED A PLACE TO WORK. HERE ARE A FEW POINTERS TO GET YOU STARTED, NO MATTER HOW SMALL YOUR WORKSPACE.

1. LIGHT
Make sure your desk is close to a source of good natural light and keep a bright desk lamp to hand so that you can keep working, even on darker evenings.

2. STORAGE
Seek out sensible storage options so that you have plenty of places to keep all your bits. But sensible doesn't have to mean ugly, it's really important that your desk is a place that inspires you to stay for long periods of time, so make it as beautiful as you can – a work of art in itself.

3. PINBOARD
Get yourself a pinboard, or stick up things that inspire you directly on your wall. Use the space right in front of you as a mini gallery and think of it as a place where you can start collections and play around with arrangements.

4. TRESTLE TABLE
Keep a trestle table to hand so that you can spread out when you need to. Trestle tables are cheap and easy to store – we'd be stuck at the Parlour without our assortment of tabletops and mix-and-match legs.

5. COMFY CHAIR AND GOOD-QUALITY STEREO
The thing about art and design is that it's best to take your time, so make sure you've got a comfy chair to work in. After all, you want to be able to enjoy the experience of sitting at your beautiful desk. In addition, there's nothing better than a never-ending sound track of new audio stimulus to get you in a creative flow, so invest in some good-quality headphones and enjoy getting lost in your own creative world.

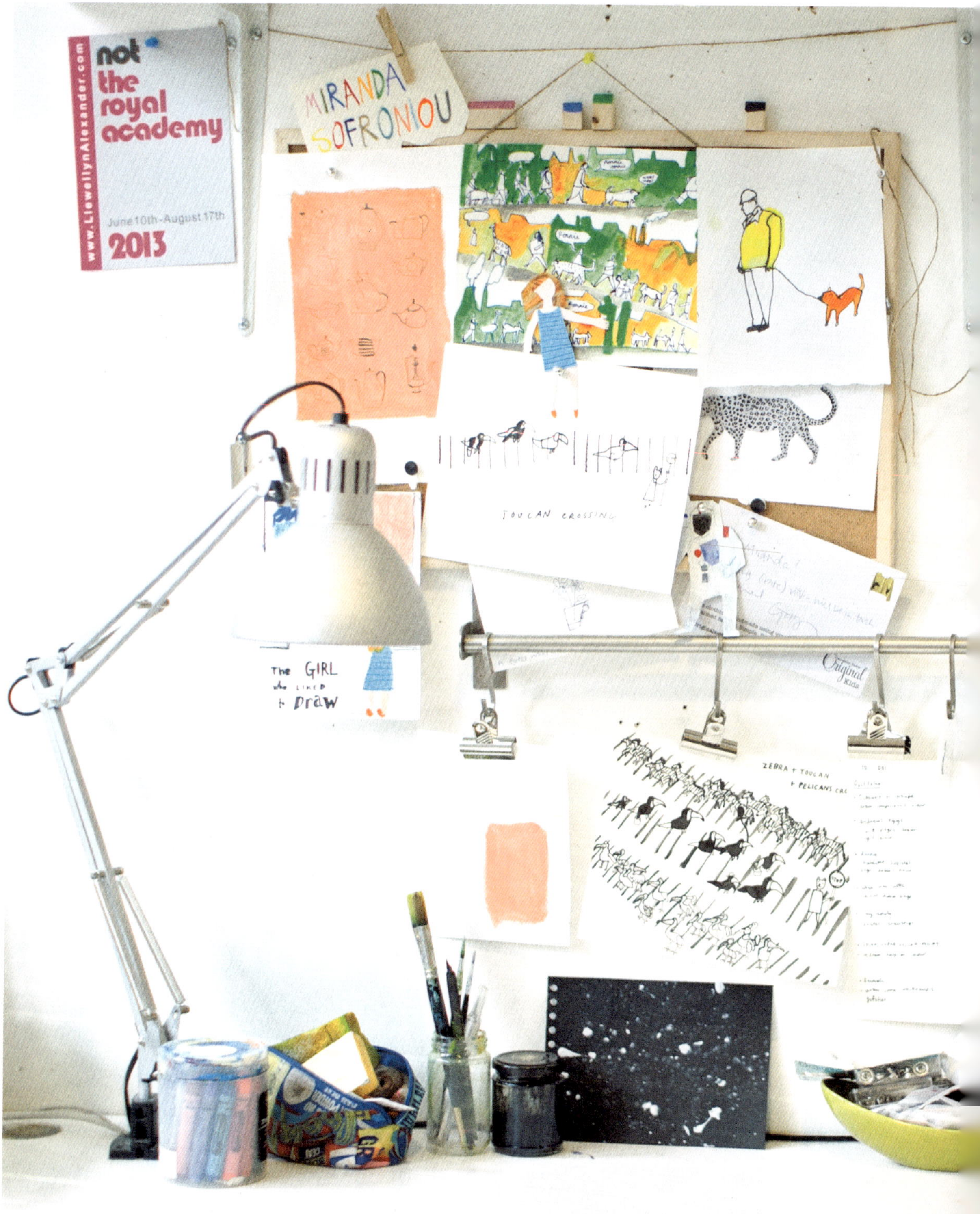
not
the
royal
academy
www.LlewellynAlexander.com
June 10th-August 17th
2013
MIRANDA
SOFRONIOU
TOUCAN CROSSING
The GIRL
who LIKED
to Draw

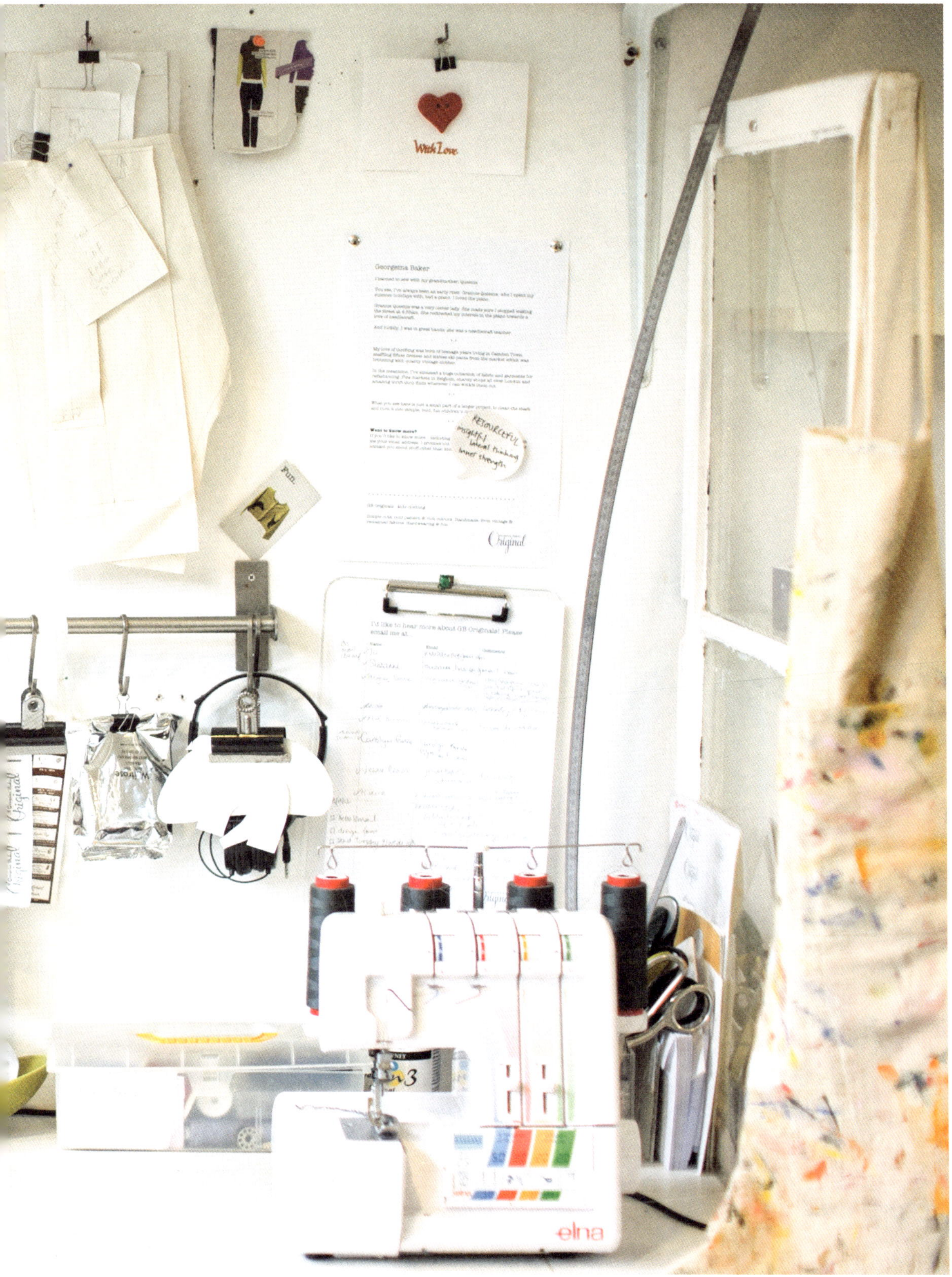
With Love
Georgeina Baker
Fun.
Original
elna

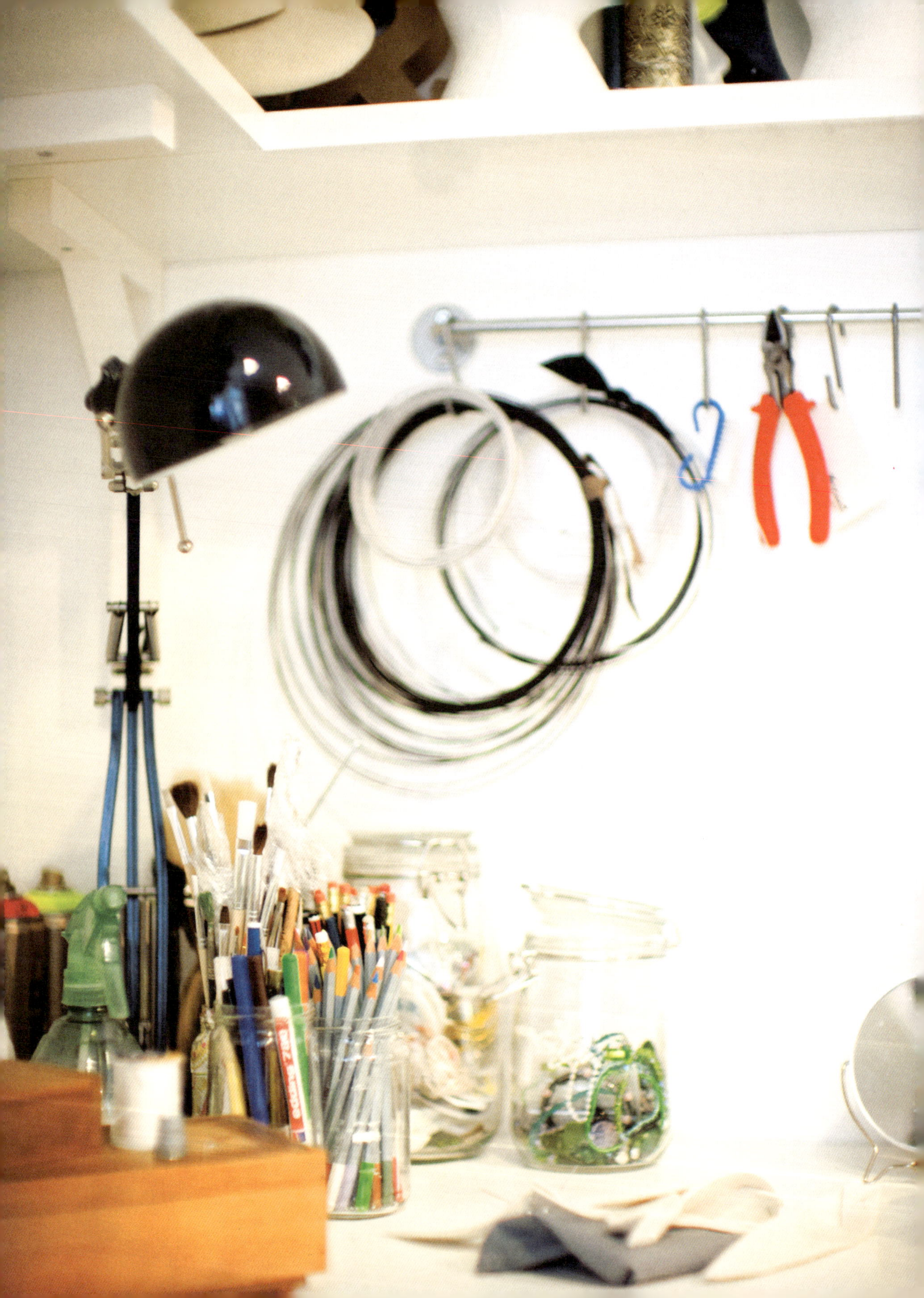

ABOUT THE PAPERED PARLOUR

× ENTER THROUGH A SMALL GREEN DOOR IN THE HEART OF SOUTH LONDON AND STEP INTO THE PAPERED PARLOUR, A CREATIVE PARADISE PACKED TO THE RAFTERS WITH NIMBLE-FINGERED ARTISTS FROM A DIVERSE RANGE OF DESIGN FIELDS.

Set up in 2009 by Claire Heafford and Louise Hall, The Papered Parlour consists of artists' studios, workshop space and an extended creative community in South London.

Home to 24 local designers, makers and creative practitioners, our co-working studio was established as a space where artists from diverse disciplines could come together to share skills and experiences. As a creative incubator, we provide peer-to-peer support for artists in the early stages of their careers along with a friendly and supportive environment in which to pursue creative practice.

As a workshop space, our varied programme of creative classes reflects our desire to create incredibly engaging learning experiences in all areas of art and design. Since 2009 we've been pushing back the limits of creative learning to get as many people as possible involved in DIY making and design. This book represents the next step in this process.

The Papered Parlour
7 Prescott Place
London
SW4 6BS

www.thepaperedparlour.co.uk

PAPERED PARLOUR TEACHERS & WORKSHOP ASSISTANTS

- Andy D'Cruz
  www.andydcruz.com
- Awon Golding
  www.awongolding.com
- Caren Hartley
  www.carenhartley.com
- Cassandra Ellis
  www.cassandraellis.co.uk
- David Webdale
  www.davidwebdale.com
- Helen Bridges
  www.helenvbridges.co.uk
- Izzy Parker
  www.izzyparker.com
- Jemma Ooi
  www.custhom.co.uk
- Jenny Gray
  www.jennifergray.co.uk
- Jenny Llewellyn
  www.jennyllewellyn.com
- Jesica Lewit
  www.jesicalewit.com
- Jonna Saarinen
  www.jonnasaarinen.com
- Judy Bentinck
  www.judybentinck.com
- Lucy Bainbridge
  www.lucybainbridge.com
- Laurie Schram
  www.laurieschram.com
- Lara Mathers
  www.yourownmadeleine.com
- Mia Jafari
  www.miajafari.com
- Natasha Moorhouse
  www.natashamoorhouse.com
- Neil Shirreff
  www.neilshirreff.com
- Rose Jackson-Taylor
  www.rosejacksontaylor.com
- Rosie Martin
  www.diy-couture.co.uk
- Ruth Lloyd
  www.ruthlloyddesign.co.uk
- Sam Roberts
  www.samrobertsphotography.co.uk
- Sarah McCartney
  www.4160tuesdays.com
- Sophie Hall
  www.sophiesorcahall.com
- Stephanie Ruben
  www.stephrubin.com

THANK YOUS

To those who have given their time and enthusiasm to make the Parlour what it is – thanks a million for your generous support.

- Alexa Montgomery
- Daniel Richards
- Elizabeth Eisen
- Emma Rowland
- Greg Piggott
- Hannah Dickson
- Hannah Armstrong
- Hannah Hull
- Hass Maricar
- Jessica Templeton Smith
- JQ Smartt
- Julia Balchin
- Kate Domash
- Katie Morris
- Kayleigh Chalcroft
- Kimi Huang
- Lauren De'Ath
- Lara Mathers
- Mandeep Dhiman
- Maria Cooper
- Marisa Molin
- Mark Stonell
- Michelle De Castro
- Naomi Waring
- Patrice Callagh
- Rachael Forde-Low
- Rosie Heafford
- Samantha Wood
- Samira Raj
- Sam McBean
- Sibylla McGrigor
- Uisliu Campbell
- Yen Tsao
- Kareena Zerefos

To our parents Joy & Adrian Heafford + Hillary & David Hall – an especially big thank you for endless support, food supplies on long days and the cheapest handyman labour in the land. Thanks also to the Parlour queen bee herself Lauren De'Ath and the silver-tongued James Marples – this book wouldn't have happened without you. Plus, a huge thank you to Pavilion for helping us to bring our book to life, to Daniel Dittmar for his graphic design flair and Johnson & Alcock for their ongoing support.

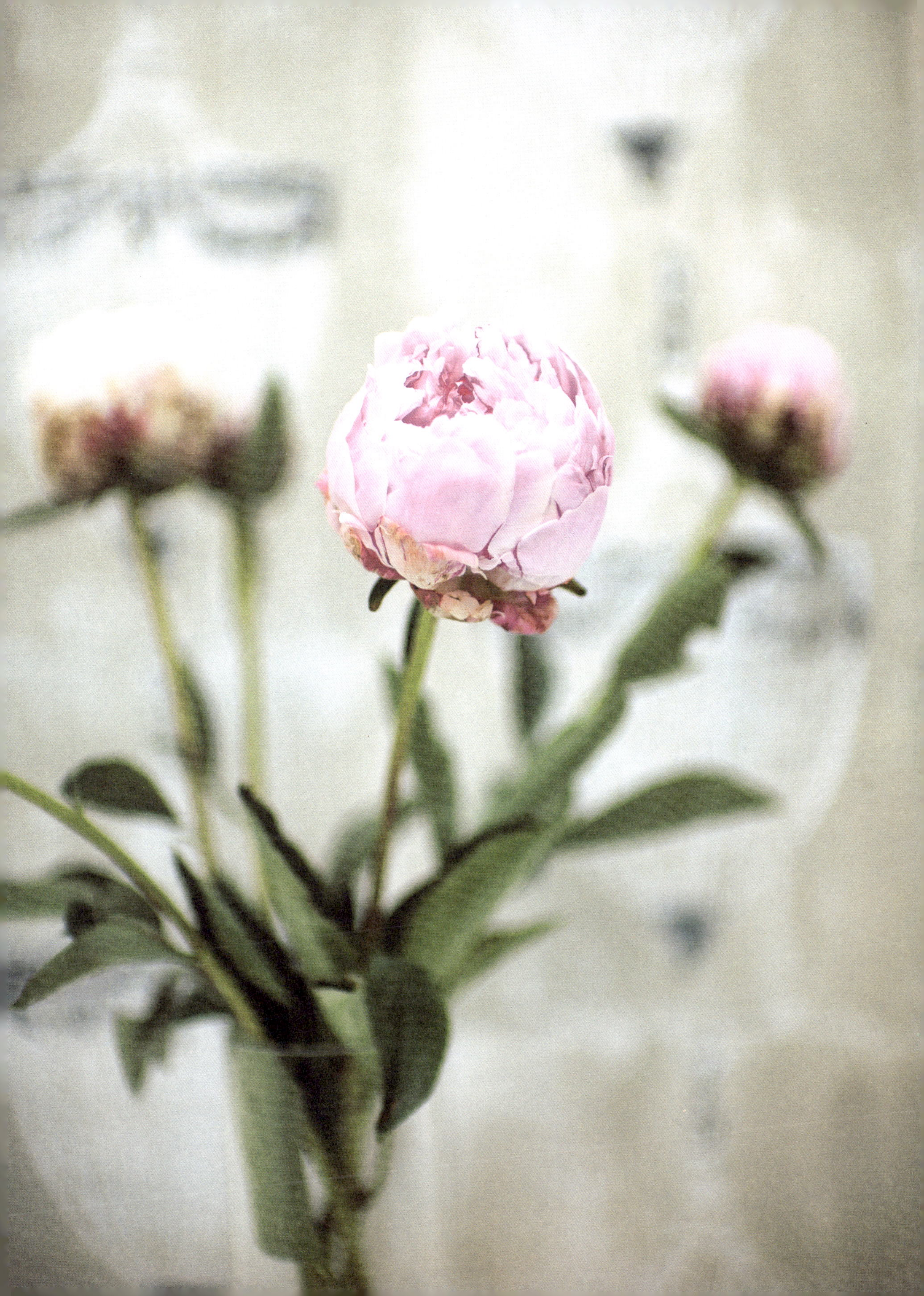

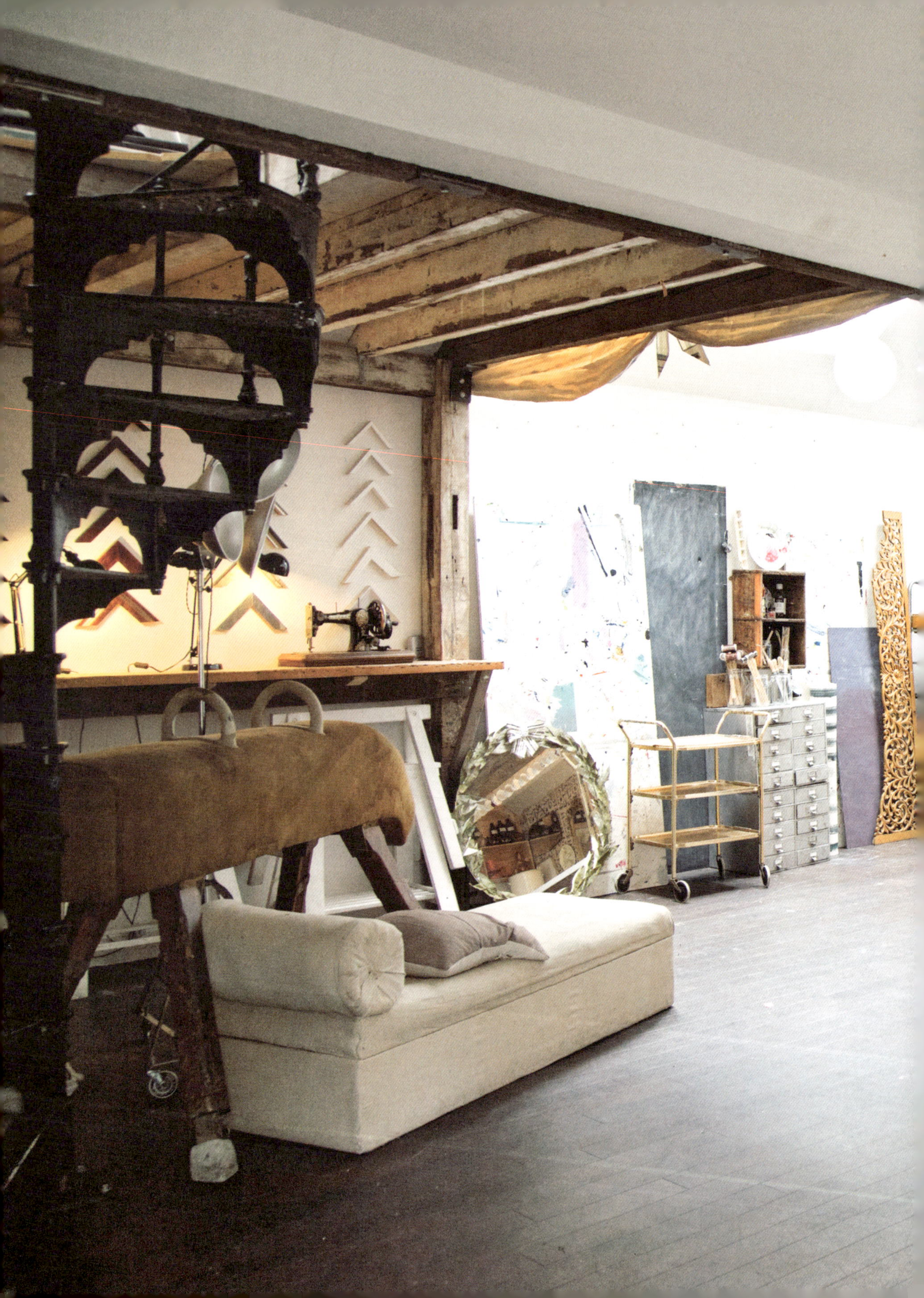

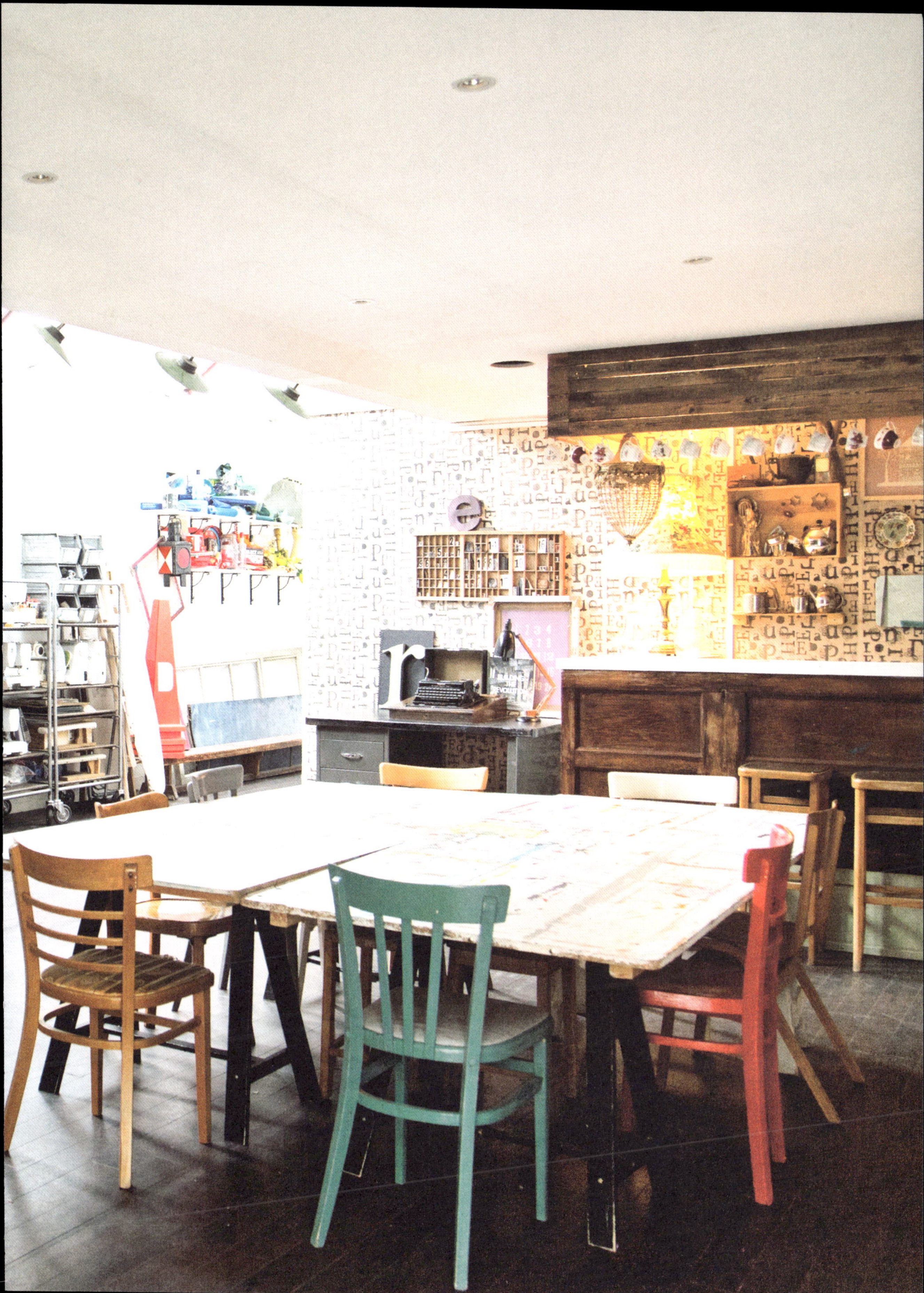

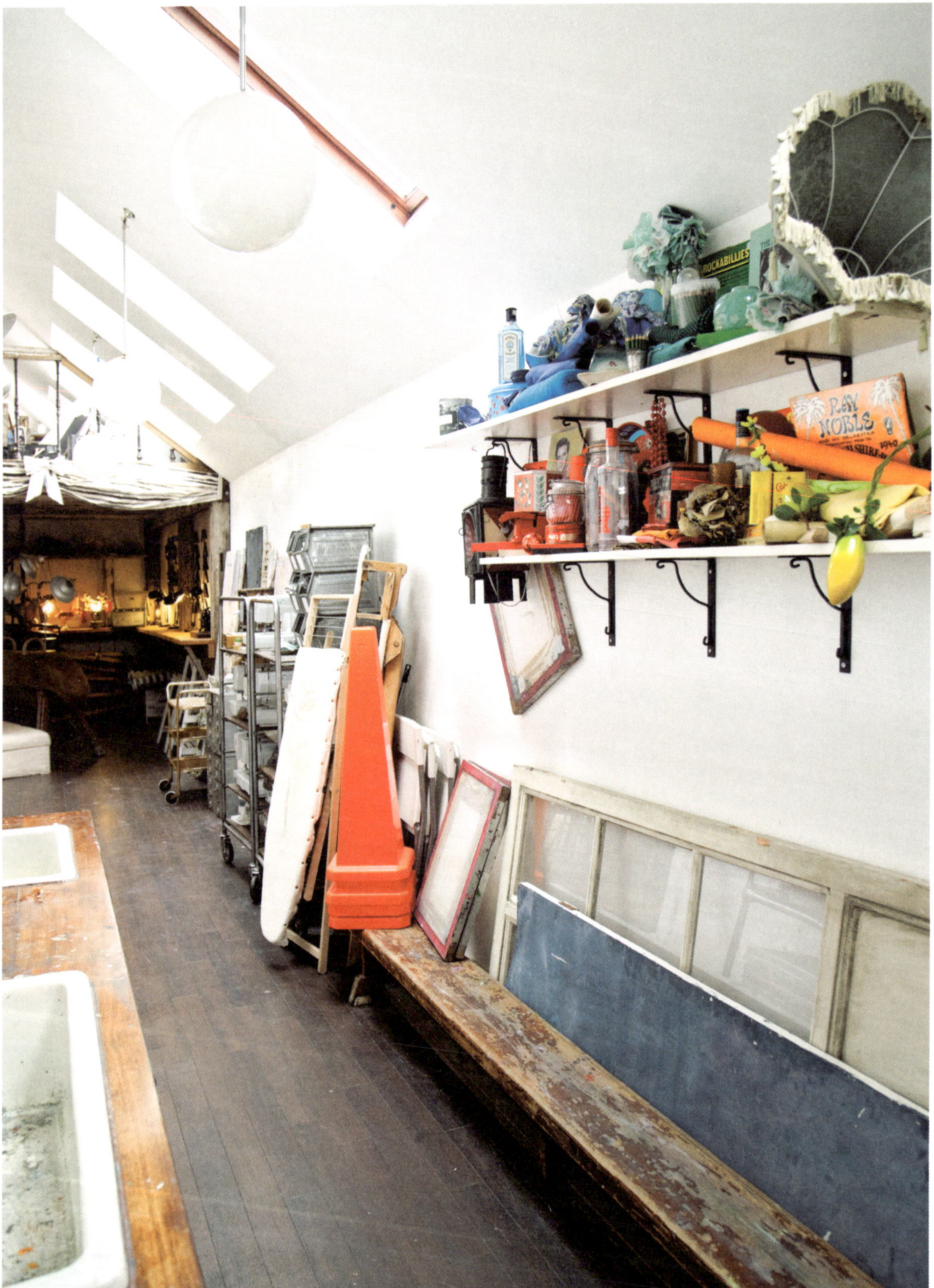
ROCKABILLIES
RAY NOBLE

INDEX

First published in the United Kingdom in 2014 by
Pavilion Books Company Limited
1 Gower Street
London
WC1E 6HD

Distributed in the United States and Canada by
Sterling Publishing Co, 387 Park Avenue South, New York,
NY 10016-8810, USA

ISBN 978-1-90981-588-9

A CIP catalogue record for this book is available from the British Library.

10 9 8 7 6 5 4 3 2 1

Reproduction by Mission, Hong Kong
Printed and bound in China by 1010 Printing International Ltd

This book can be ordered direct from the publisher at
www.pavilionbooks.com